A Killer
Appetite

# A Killer Appetite

*Overcoming My Eating Disorder
and the Thinking That Fed It*

HOLLY PENNEBAKER

*Jefferson, North Carolina*

ISBN (print) 978-1-4766-7869-6 ∞
ISBN (ebook) 978-1-4766-3764-8

LIBRARY OF CONGRESS AND BRITISH LIBRARY
CATALOGUING DATA ARE AVAILABLE

Cover photographs by Paige Pederzani

Printed in the United States of America

Toplight is an imprint of McFarland & Company, Inc., Publishers

*Box 611, Jefferson, North Carolina 28640
www.toplightbooks.com*

# Table of Contents

# Acknowledgments

Thank you, Gabby Bernstein, for showing me that F.E.A.R. = False Evidence Appearing Real, and for showing me how to separate fact from fiction. Your work challenged my thinking and actions, which helped me to choose love over fear, to forgive others and myself, to find gratitude no matter what, and to never stop believing in miracles.

Thank you, Whitney Cummings, for being you and for sharing your authentic, talented self with others. You've taught me to respect myself and honor my personality, to cherish humor, to fall in love with laughter and to be stronger than the challenges I face. From you, I've learned that I CAN and WILL find happiness through humor, and it's OK if some jokes fall flat. I've used your TV shows, standup acts, and your book to accept and love my sarcastic sense of humor that's drier than the Sahara. Because of you, I'm able to be more real with

**Meeting Whitney Cummings (left) was on my bucket list. I checked it off after her show in Chicago on October 19, 2017.**

vii

myself and more real with others, and I'm also able to love myself and love others. And hey, Whitney, *I'm fine* too.

Thank you, Fred DeVito, for always saying "yes." From my friendship with you, I've learned the importance of generosity, an open mind and kindness. You and Elisabeth provide a beautiful shining light to others, which because of your spirits and grace will never go dim. Your Core Fusion fitness and yoga classes may have changed my body, but most important, they changed my mindset. Your work has given me the gift of peace, and the will to get stronger.

Thank you, Mrs. Anna "Mama" Keefe, for being the most memorable teacher I could ever ask for. Your tough, military-inspired teaching style for Lexington Traditional Magnet School's 8th grade language arts class sparked my passion for words, writing, grammar, sentence structure, punctuation, and 87 pronouns each student had to memorize and recite out loud in class.

**"Mama Keefe" and "little Holly" at my middle school promotion ceremony in June 1996.**

Your class was hard, but it prepared students for the real world and empowered us to find confidence, build an unbreakable work ethic and aspire to make a difference. You believed in me, you pushed me to do "my best and then some," and you helped me realize my potential. Your homework assignments commonly seemed unreasonably difficult, if not impossible, but they equipped me with the determination needed to succeed as a professional editor and, now, a published author.

## Special Thank You to the Editor

The first time I met Mike Reilley was in 2010, just outside his office door at DePaul University. He shamelessly tossed his knowledge-filled head from left to right, over and over, signaling that what I knew about sports coverage wasn't anything like what I'd learn in his journalism and sports reporting classes. No, sir.

Mike was intimidating. And he knew it! I realized within the first two seconds of meeting him, and witnessing the assertive, take-no-shit headshake, that I'd NEVER want to be on the guy's bad side. But sure enough, during my journalism program at DePaul, I found myself there. I cried when he yelled at me for being late to an open study hall (I didn't think the hours were a hard start and finish). He yelled at me when I told him I'd correct 70 percent of the edits he made on one of my multimedia stories, and I cried again (note: ALWAYS correct 100 percent of your editor's revisions).

He was tough, and on many days, Mike was one scary editor.

Don't ever turn in assignments past deadline. Don't ever interrupt Mike; save questions for when he finishes talking. Be highly vigilant of what you live tweet in class and what might not be appropriate. Don't ever lie—he'll find out the truth.

Mike sent me to crime-ridden neighborhoods to tell stories that would help improve those communities. He's the reason I found myself in Chicago's Dirksen Federal Building in 2011, breaking the news of the Rod Blagojevich sentencing, and then on a live segment with a Milwaukee radio station. He's the reason I covered the unveiling of Chicago's Divvy Bike Share Program. He selected me to tell a heroic firefighter's unforgettable story about racing to Ground Zero on September 11, 2001, to help in any way he was needed. And Mike is the MOST SIGNIFICANT person in my professional development.

Despite how strict, grueling and fearsome Mike was, I never once hesitated to share my raw, personal story with him—first and second drafts, nonetheless. I showed him my vulnerability, my shame and my emotional wounds. I trusted Mike's nonjudgmental approach, unmistaken ability to leave no typo unturned, and the support he provided during my time in treatment and time spent finalizing each chapter.

Present day, we laugh and catch up over pizza or tacos, and the occasional beer if we're in the same city. Mike's become one heck of a mentor and friend. He's held my hand along the way and I'll be forever grateful that he has my back. This book would never have happened without Mike's support, and his ability to edit content like no one I've ever known.

Mike is a Society of Professional Journalists/Google News Initiative digital tools trainer who has trained more than 4,500 journalists nationwide on how to build interactive stories. He teaches data and multimedia journalism at the University of Illinois–Chicago. A former reporter at the *Los Angeles Times* and web editor at the *Chicago Tribune*, Mike served for 13 years as a faculty member at Northwestern University, Arizona State University and DePaul University, teaching digital journalism to hundreds of students and professional journalists. He holds journalism degrees from the University of Nebraska–Lincoln (undergrad) and Northwestern University (master's). Mike founded and updates the research site The Journalist's Toolbox for SPJ (www.journaliststoolbox.org) and founded the digital training company Penny Press Digital, LLC.

**Mike Reilley teaches writing and editing for digital platforms.**

# CHAPTER 1

# The trigger was pulled…

… on a Friday afternoon at work inside my Cincinnati office, the second I saw on Twitter that an edible cookie dough shop had opened up in New York City.

The irresistibly sweet, one-of-a-kind cookie dough taste took over my mind and I knew that when I got home that evening, I would devour an obscene amount of cookie dough. I also knew that once I'd satisfied my suddenly-there sweet tooth, I'd feel debilitating pain, unbearable regret and enough shame to destroy anything and everything productive, social or fun that weekend.

On the mid–July afternoon when the downfall was initiated, only a few colleagues were working in my office in Cincinnati's Over the Rhine neighborhood.

"Oh no way, you guys, look! A cookie dough shop in NYC that serves cookie dough as if it's ice cream!"

My colleagues looked at photos on my monitor as I scrolled through the shop's Twitter feed, marveling at the cookie dough-turned-art. A scoop of cookie dough served in an ice cream cone, two scoops served in a dish with creatively-designed frosting patterns, and New Yorkers enjoying cookie dough offered in more ways than I'd ever seen.

**I can't remember my colleagues' reactions … because my soul was no longer there.**

My thoughts began racing: the errand I had to run after work, the 6 p.m. yoga class I'd committed to (and needed), and anything else that could get in the way of my "killer" cookie dough consumption.

The errand took longer than I'd expected, and I arrived to the yoga studio just in the nick of time. The class that Friday evening was yin yoga—rather calming and restorative with slow transitions between passive postures.

Even though yin yoga isn't necessarily a challenging class when it comes to balancing, I was all over the place. I was off. Big time. I couldn't focus, I couldn't be present during the hour, and although my body was there, my mind and heart were in the future—planning the grocery store run that would secure my massive measure of cookie dough and enable binge-eating bliss later that night.

Once class wrapped up, I felt my heartbeat start to gain speed and my mind start to fog. Only one thing was clear: I must get to the one grocery store that would have everything I needed to satisfy that night's binge, and where it would be the "safest" place to buy such an absurd selection of food.

Really, all I needed was the tub of the Cookie Dough Café brand edible cookie dough, which the Oakley neighborhood's Fresh Market sold. But with that one item came the need for ice cream too. And a frozen pizza. And shredded cheese to top the pizza because manufactures never add "enough." The Fresh Market was the best bet for the binge-eating shopping spree, as I was least likely to run into a friend, acquaintance or other familiar face. They'd more likely be at the nearby Whole Foods or common chain stores located conveniently in the neighborhood. But no one I know shops at the Fresh Market, so that means that's where that Friday night would take me.

By the time I've entered the store, my heartbeat is at an uncomfortable, rapid pace. My emotions and ability to think rationally are stripped. Self-awareness is out the door. My thoughts race like horses that have just been let out the gates, like the voice of my eating disorder is yelling, "Go, baby, go!"

I need to buy a combination of food that looks more "normal" so that the cashier doesn't judge me or pick up on the fact that this food is for an abnormal eating practice.

*Here's what I'll do: I'll buy a few good produce items so they'll balance out the bad items in my shopping cart and my purchase will resemble a very common grocery shopping errand that could very easily take place on any given Friday night.*

*OK, organic bananas, organic kale, organic romaine and fresh fruit. Done.*

But I can't get too caught up in the healthy choices that mask the binge-eating grocery purchase. I must make sure I get everything I need to satisfy the binge, because only if I'm fully satisfied will the craving go away, and maybe, just maybe, it will be my very last unhealthy, out-of-control eating episode.

*Cookie dough ... ice cream ... pizza ... cheese (over and over again in my head). But wait, cheddar snack crackers sound good. No way— they're almost five bucks—not happening. OK, back to my list—that will be enough ... for tonight. Four things, Holly, focus. Focus.*

⌒⌒

I need to make smart spending choices. The Fresh Market is rather expensive, after all, and I gotta binge on a budget. Every little bit counts when you're a 30-something, single Cincinnati girl financially supporting yourself.

*There's Halo Top brand, which doesn't come with the guilt of other brands ... but tonight, I want to go all out. Graeter's chocolate chip ice cream would be the best—they put huge chunks of chocolate in each pint. Whoa, hold up—the Fresh Market charges $7 per pint?! Forget that—I can get a pint of Graeter's at Kroger for $4.99. There's Ben and Jerry's for $4.99—that could work. But no, they don't have just chocolate chip, they only have chocolate chip cookie dough and because I'm going all out and because it has to be the perfect binge, I want the entire tub of cookie dough mixed with a pint of chocolate chip ice cream that has no other cookie dough besides what comes in the tub I'm buying. Another option: Home-made Brand—a favorite since I was a kid. They offer a 1.5-liter tub of chocolate chip ice cream for $6.49, which would be the best deal. But I can't go that route because then I'll have nearly an entire gallon of ice cream at home with absolutely no self-control to go with it. Bad idea.*

*This mental process (aka nightmare) repeats four to five times as my eyes stare at the freezer in a complete trance ... my heartbeat is as fast as I can handle and no other thought can permeate the current rotation going on. It's a complete tornado, and I'm sure my face shows the pressure, panic and agony.*

⌒⌒

I hope I don't see anyone I know. I'll have to explain why I'm here and then they'll see what's in my shopping cart, and then they'll be able to tell that something's wrong. They'll see the panic in my eyes, they'll notice it in my body language, and they'll hear it in my voice as it awkwardly shakes when I try to speak.

They'll catch me at my most vulnerable state, and they will discover that I don't have my shit together, and that I'm falling apart from a mental illness that's slowly worked at destroying my life for the past 15 years.

*I can't do it. I cannot see anyone I know.*

*Don't look around, Holly. Don't look around…*

I arrived home to breathe only a partial sigh of relief because, sure enough, I was safe from running into "so-and-so" at the grocery store, but the relief was interrupted by the wind tunnel that blew my body, mind and soul up to my third-floor condo and dangerously into a storm of raging, unruly, uncontrollable food consumption.

About halfway though the usual amount of ice cream and cookie dough I put away, something different happened: I started crying so hard that I couldn't breathe. **I sobbed, aware that neighbors might hear me through the walls, but unafraid because this was literally my cry for help.**

There was no enjoyment of the mixture of ice cream and cookie dough that I'd come to believe would never let me down. I gagged looking down at the bowl in my lap, and moved it aside to the coffee table. I held my face and forehead deep into my hands and uncontrollably wept. My body slid onto the floor, my legs drew into my core and my arms moved from my legs to my head to my shoulders as I tried to find comfort and to get a grip.

I was having a perilous panic attack. The tears poured and dripped onto my clothing and living room floor. I couldn't swallow. Each scream and gasp for air was the final attempt to get through the attack on my own without calling 911. I'd reached a point of terror I'd never experienced during a binge episode. It felt like what dying a painful death would feel like. And it wouldn't stop.

"I need help."

"I can't control my eating."

"I can't deal with this on my own and I don't know how to."

"I can't stop hurting myself."

"This is the source of anxiety and depression, embarrassment and pain, and self-doubt that is much bigger than me."

"I just want to be normal and have a healthy relationship with food."

After about an hour, I was all cried out. I couldn't yet breathe steadily, and eerie tremors rushed from head to toe. My vision was blurred and my headache could have put a crack in my skull. I had trouble breaking through the panic attack's paralysis, but no matter what, I had to find help. I wasn't even sure I was alive during parts of that hour of pure horror.

I was 34 years old when I realized my call for help could save me from death.

I couldn't fight the 15-year battle with food on my own any longer.

I was raised in Lexington, Kentucky, and never struggled with depression, anxiety, obsessive-compulsive disorder or an eating disorder until I began college.

My college years at the University of Kentucky introduced me to plenty of pressure that one should almost expect during that time. The need to perform well in school, the need to be liked and socially accepted, the need to be pretty (cue clothes, cosmetics, hairspray, tanning, body wrapping, plastic surgery ... the WORKS), the need to make money to support myself and have fun, and, in my experience, the "need" to compete in a fitness competition.

The pressure I experienced in college was all too new. My expectations of myself spiked higher than the top of the Empire State Building. I couldn't even be sure where my new standards of "acceptable" had come from.

I had one of those picture-perfect childhoods. There was no literal white picket fence, but figuratively speaking, it lined my quiet neighborhood yard without flaw, just outside the quaint dogwood trees that lined the driveway. I grew up an only child, surrounded by immediate family, friends, teammates and an unforgettable church youth group camaraderie. I was smothered in love and support. Hopes and dreams dazzled every single day (this book making the number two spot). I believed I was capable of achieving any and every goal—that success, abundance and love would never be too far out of reach.

As I transitioned into the professional workforce in my early 20s, working in Chicago's high fashion market, it was *that* era when I realized my passion is with words and writing rather than runways and couture, and so I went to graduate school and earned a master's degree in journalism within 14 months.

I took DePaul University's grad school program

I was named "Miss Liberty" in kindergarten in 1987 and earned a special spot in the yearbook for academics and student leadership.

very seriously and devoted all my focus to being successful (like extra credit/honor roll/A+ success) in each class, gaining experience and knowledge I'd need to hit the ground running, especially in an infamous industry of cut-throat competition, back-breaking pressure and outrageous demands.

The lack of balance left plenty of time for me to be alone ... and plenty of time to "enjoy" food ... although I wasn't enjoying food. I was eating very little, and then binge eating in place of friends and social support, as a substitute to reward my hard work and to fill the emptiness I experienced at that time.

Part of that I must credit to an internship with one of Chicago's top news stations. It was my first role in a newsroom, and the internship

**Friends and fellow grads Amber Tweedie (left) and Fatimah Aramide Salami with me on graduation day, June 12, 2011, at Allstate Arena.**

introduced me to the intensity of journalism, including its grueling hours. I arrived to work by 3:30 a.m. and left around noon. I couldn't figure out when to incorporate meals and snacks, or sleep and rest. My body never adjusted, no matter how hard I tried to fall asleep by 6:30 p.m. so I could get eight hours of sleep before the madness began. Even when I felt hungry, I wasn't sure if I should eat a meal, have a snack, or if my stomach was disguising exhaustion with hunger. By the time the weekend rolled around (I was lucky enough to have Saturday and Sunday off), I was running on only a few hours of sleep per night, and I was simply shutting down. I was too drained and weak to prepare a meal, and my financial frugality kept me from paying for delivery. Looking back, it's a fatigue that literally hurts, that's impossible to "tough through." I lost weight, I lost strength, and I became obsessed with trying to recharge my energy.

I started canceling weekend plans, no matter how much fun they would be, because I couldn't gather enough get-up-and-go to shower and get dressed for a night out, hail a cab and be energetically in the moment with friends. I'd become an absolute dud. I will forever kick myself for choosing to skip a 2012 Steve Aoki concert. I crawled into bed at 8:30 that night instead of dancing the night away. I repeat—I was a career-obsessed dud.

I stayed dedicated to the news grind and within six months of graduating in December 2011, I accepted a position at a major news station in Atlanta. My mental health challenges were along for the ride, and stayed with me through nearly two years in Georgia's capital city. My shift in Atlanta was from noon to 9 p.m., and then, after about a year, a change in my role and responsibilities moved me to the 5 a.m. to 2 p.m. shift.

These two years in Atlanta marked a time when yoga and working

**The 11Alive News morning team together on set, likely before sunrise, September 25, 2013.**

out emerged as my top priorities outside of work, and my discovery of exhale Spa's magical Core Fusion and yoga programs came at an impeccable time, when life outside of work was off balance and quite empty. Because the instructors gave me an incredibly wonderful feeling each visit, I usually took class five or six days per week, routinely taking two classes back to back.

The empowerment and motivation I felt from exhale drove me through each week and helped me keep my head up. The exhale community and its belief in mind-body transformation made tough times easier to handle (and when you work in news and live with an eating disorder, there are plenty of tough times). After a few months, I'd built community with the teachers and clients at exhale, along with friendships and support. I felt stronger, but not strong enough to win the fight against mental illness.

When I accepted an offer at a Cincinnati news station in September 2013, my issues came with me to the Midwest. I became the station's health and fitness writer, which meant I had to look the part, play the part and exhibit expertise in healthy living.

"No days off" was the rule. If I took a day off from working out, it meant that I wasn't working hard enough, that I missed out on progress I would have made by working out. Expectations of fitness regimen and dieting had gotten so unrealistic. I ate a chicken breast and a lightly-dressed mixed green salad every single night during my 3:30 p.m.–12:30 a.m. work shift. Between my inability to meet those impossible expectations, and the pain of failed relationships with colleagues at that station, the "I'm not good enough" belief really took its toll on my well-being.

My next career step took me out of news and placed me on the content team of a human capital executive association in January 2017, working in digital content production and editing, program management, and hosting podcasts and webinars.

I was also teaching yoga on the side after earning my certification in June 2015. That also happened during the "I'm not good enough" era … the era that's still going strong.

There I was: 34 years old and wanting so much more from life than what I had earned so far. I was dwelling on more desires than my anxiety could handle. I have no spouse, no children, and I don't own a home. I have very few friends, and even fewer that I've kept a long relationship with.

However, I have a checked-off to-do list for every week, and a list ready for each day of the following week. I have a kitchen cabinet containing my alphabetized spices, straight tread lines from the vacuum cleaner maintained on the carpet, a clothes closet organized by color, season and shirt sleeve length, and books stacked from largest to smallest in size. Even my sock drawer is impeccable.

I also have a tendency to fight depression, envy, worry, fear, an eating disorder, and, well … anything and everything opposite relaxation and freedom. More often than not, I've questioned a serious clinical problem when it comes to evaluating my mental state. How could I possibly be so sad, uncomfortable and insecure?

No matter where I was living, what demands I was working to meet, what ups and downs were happening in life, my eating disorder and other mental health struggles were there all along.

The issues prompted many visits to a handful of different therapists and psychiatrists over the years. As if they'd jumped from a dark corner and appeared right before my eyes, medications had become a part of my daily vitamin intake. And I didn't even want to take the prescribed medicines. I wanted to get better—to feel better—thanks to my own inner strength and some mental help from professional practitioners. The fact that I had to swallow a pill once a day made me feel even worse. The way I interpreted it, taking medicine every day meant I was weak, odd, problematic and simply messed up. I wasn't able to believe that it's OK to not be OK, and I wasn't able to internally separate from the stigma I mistakenly attached to taking medicine for mental health.

There was always a little voice telling me I was out of control, but it wasn't until that final night of eating disorder terror and panic that I finally reached for the phone.

I grabbed hold of my phone tightly and looked online for Cincinnati eating disorder help. The first search result caught my eye: Eating Disorder Treatment Center of Cincinnati (EDTC), located just a couple miles away. There were more than 10 centers and doctors to choose from, but something about the EDTC just felt right. With zero hesitation, I tapped the "Schedule for a Free Consultation" bar at the bottom of the mobile site.

It was a tiny first step, but the relief that rushed over me was very powerful—I breathed a different kind of air and my heart felt a warm blanket of support.

Within just a few days, I'd scheduled an appointment and found myself in the cozy office of an assessment specialist, Mallory, unloading details about the earliest signs of unhealthy eating patterns up to the present day. Mallory provided a level of comfort that allowed me to drop all fear of being judged, and feeling ugly and weak. I was able to remain calm and open, and, most of all, honest.

She asked when my most recent binge episode was. I shifted into a lower, quieter voice as I resentfully admitted to putting away an entire pizza the night before—meaning it was less than 24 hours between my binge and my assessment.

Talking to Mallory marked the first realization that I had, without a doubt, reached out for help. I'm a long-version explainer, and she did an awesome job of not only staying engaged, but also recording my dialogue by typing notes into my online assessment form. She took my weight, but said it was a blind measurement that was purposefully kept from me as part of the routine assessment. That part didn't bother me in the slightest. I've always been cool with the scale's reading. From the outside, no one could tell I struggle with an eating disorder (little did I know, no one ever *looks like* they have an eating disorder).

*Author's note: The name of the treatment center has been replaced with an anonymous name, Eating Disorder Treatment Center of Cincinnati (EDTC), to protect the organization's privacy.*

# CHAPTER 2

# History of Binge Eating
## *You* Have *to Eat This Way*

I was 19 years old when I first took notice of binge-eating behavior. Along with being a full-time college student and part-time receptionist, I was training to compete in a fitness competition, which seemed like a third job. My trainer had transformed my diet according to a plan that was so incredibly strict, detailed and, well, quite addictive. I started removing the yolks before scrambling eggs, the crust from pizza and replacing cookies with carrots. My trainer held me accountable for maintaining a diet designed to win a fitness competition. However, my own voice inside my head was responsible for the unrealistic self-pressure I had begun putting on myself when it came to eating.

*You have to eat this way, Holly. You have to be the best eater. If you're not the best eater, you won't win the fitness competition. Everyone else is going to be eating according to this type of diet so you have to as well. And you have to eat better than they eat—you have to be the best at every aspect of training so you can win. Coming in second place is not an option.*

It'd become fairly customary to eat a chicken breast for breakfast because it was the best source of lean protein—critical for a fitness competitor. My life revolved around meal times and workouts. No wonder relationships failed back then. All I talked about was the gym. A group of friends invited me along for a trip to Cincinnati's Kings Island amusement park, and we all split a couple pizzas for lunch. I was ridiculed for eating only the sauce, cheese and toppings. No bread for this girl. Their making fun of me came from a good place of kindness, but I couldn't help feeling like the nerd in the lunchroom who got picked on in school. I'd become so consumed by the competition that the thought of eating pizza crust pushed me too close to believing that because I ate the crust, I wouldn't be the winner.

Once a week, my meal plan allowed a cheat meal. I was introduced to the cheat meal concept for the first time as part of my training. For one meal, once per week, as part of my heavily-restricted diet, I was given permission to eat whatever I wanted in one sitting. I'd held myself from pizza, a burger and fries, ice cream, lasagna, many "off-limits" foods, and when it came time for the cheat meal, I'd eat whichever "off-limit" food I was most craving. I remember the cheat meal most often came from a fast food joint's drive-thru window, and was made up of a cheeseburger, a large order of fries and an ice cream sundae (hold the whipped cream).

This practice went on for months. As time went on, the cheat meal slowly grew in size, and it also grew in importance. I started thinking about the cheat meal and planning for it days in advance. I looked forward to the meal with much more enthusiasm than food should ever create.

Before I got the chance to compete, I had surgery on my left foot. And so after months of work and dedication ... with no warning ... the show was over. However, I'd gained serious muscle mass and felt very strong.

I kept the fitness competitor diet going. I loved how it had transformed my physique, lifted my confidence and gave me courage.

A few weeks after the operation, my recovery took a turn for the worse. Long story short, my body wouldn't heal properly and I was bedridden for a year and two months, with the possibility of losing two of my toes. My foot had to be elevated above my heart at all times—24 hours per day. I was unable to be active, and my training came to a screeching halt.

There was no longer a fitness competition to work for, but over the year-plus of recovery, I never halted the food addiction I'd gained in return. I was obsessed with food and the choices that came with eating it. **My black-and-white personality didn't allow me to see foods in any way other than good or bad, and at that time, it was my goal to eat as well as possible.**

Over time, that goal became influenced by the college life—nights of cramming for exams over fast food, nights of bashes and drinking until I found a bar to dance on or I blacked out (or both), sporting events, spring breaks, pool parties and plenty of reasons to be in good shape. It was a significant image-conscious period of life.

Eventually, the cheat meals blended in with my regular eating and no longer were a planned part of my week. I didn't think about protein, vegetables or balance because my priorities were not well aligned with a healthy lifestyle. As a college sophomore, I thought the cool thing to do was to pay little attention to nutritious food choices, to be able to drink and party with the best of 'em, and to see no change in my body—to be fit and thin no matter what. And I thought I was doing just that—I was full of confidence early in college. I'd been exposed to more fun than I ever thought possible coming from a sheltered high school experience, and I was having the time of my life. And to prove it, I still have the butterfly tattoo on my hip that seemed like *such* a good idea during sophomore year's spring break in Daytona Beach (along with a few other bad decisions).

However, there was something going on inside that fun, free-spirited 19-year-old girl that I didn't realize was a step in a terribly wrong direction. **My poor eating choices were about to turn into a big, scary monster.**

I put on weight. It was the "freshman 15" (that came my sophomore year), and on someone as petite as me, it was noticeable. In fact, a friend pointed it out to me when she saw photos of me in a bikini from that year's spring break trip. Another friend mentioned my swollen stomach when I had on a fitted shirt. Even my own father joked about the semi-tire that I had begun carrying around my waist.

The comments honestly didn't bother me. Maybe my confidence back then was enough to keep me above the negative influence they could have had … or *maybe* I was comfortable in my own skin.

Eventually, my vulnerability, self-assurance and awareness of my diet sang a new, sad song.

The tune called on my cheat meals to come back around, and I'm not even sure how, exactly, I once again became conscious of my eating. The cheat meal became a reward, and it also took place when a hangover started to wear off, after a highly stressful day, or when I knew a huge exam was only a few days away.

My cheat meals had grown into gigantic portions. One meal didn't even cut it. I'd swing through fast food restaurants' drive-thru windows and leave with two meals *and* a dessert. I wanted to make sure the cheat meal was satisfying enough to get the craving out of my system, so that when I finished eating, there could be no way that I'd want more food.

This was my sophomore year of college, and although the cheat meals weren't a regular thing, they never stopped happening for years to come.

Years later when I lived in Atlanta, a binge-eating episode occurred in late summer of 2012—the memory perfectly clear even now. I spent the early afternoon with some friends, just hanging out at a nearby apartment, taking it easy. I had to work the next morning (unexpectedly on a Sunday), and they all wanted to go out to a couple bars that night. I knew they'd want to stay out too late for me since I had to be up early the next day, ready for a full shift of work. I guess I could have gone out for just a little while, but thanks to black-and-white thinking, that thought never crossed my mind. It had to be a full, epic night out, or nothing at all.

In all reality, I wanted something other than company and a night at a bar anyway—it wasn't cutting it for me that weekend. So I parted ways for the day, and with the repeated anxiety and panic that comes with a binge-eating episode, I picked up a large, extra cheese pizza from Mellow Mushroom, ice cream from my favorite Publix grocery store ... and because I dare not pass it up ... a cookie sandwich from the Publix bakery (two chocolate chip cookies with frosting in the middle, and then more frosting that makes a smiley face on the side of the sandwich).

I ate about three-fourths of the pizza, about half the tub of ice cream, and just two bites of the cookie sandwich before my stomach started ripping in half. The pain had me leaning up against the fridge, unable to breathe, unable to move. I stood there, slouched over, grabbing to my belly and lower back, begging out loud for the pain to subside. I might never forget that episode—I might never be able to. If I remember correctly, I called off from work the next day because I felt sick, overcome by guilt and unable to face my colleagues, let alone perform my job. The pain and shame were just too strong.

My isolation, black-and-white thinking and binge-eating tendency had become the reason why I'd often find Saturday nights spent alone inside the walls of a spotless home more appealing than fun, fabulous nights out. I didn't want to get dressed up, meet people or make new memories…. **I didn't deserve any of it … not while I had my binge-eating secret stashed away**.

That was 2012. It's now 2017 and my pep talk has been repeated more times than I can count.

*You have to stop this, Holly. You can no longer eat like this. It's doing nothing for you. It's giving you nothing. You're better than this. You're too good to fall. You're too strong to give into this bad habit. The bad habit hurts so badly. It tears your stomach and soul apart.*

*But I can't tell where the urges come from and when they're going to hit too hard to resist. When I feel the need to binge, I cannot put it to rest. I have to satisfy my food craving, and if I don't, I can't think clearly because the craving has consumed my every thought.*

*Stop doing it, Holly! Just stop! Please! Just stop! Who are you?!*

And as my own coach and as my true self, my pep talk wasn't good enough. I gave in to my craving more often than not, no matter how badly it hurt.

No one ever knew this, but each year, Independence Day had its own unique meaning for me. Each July 4 would certainly be a celebration—a time when we proudly honor our nation and celebrate a life of freedom. But, as I'd come to recognize my binge-eating disorder and food addiction over a 15-year span, it was also the day I'd claim independence from my eating disorder—freedom from binge eating. Or so I thought.

Something else had happened plenty of times—the traditional binge-eating episode and emotional breakdown on July 3. I mean, I had to have a last meal, right?

Then, behind closed doors, on each and every July 4, I'd make the promise to myself to once again start a very restrictive diet that included only the healthiest of food choices. No more cheats, no more regrets—freedom from the pain. Independence Day would be the day that I'd declare independence from my eating disorder and food addiction.

Also behind closed doors, each year, I'd eventually reach the point of failure. The restrictions I'd place on my diet and the elimination of so many different foods proposed a plan that was impossible to follow.

It wasn't realistic. It wasn't healthy. And by no means was it symbolic of freedom.

Fitness and yoga are part of my everyday schedule. Hands down, "they have to be." Besides, I'd been active all my life, and that could never change.

A grueling hour with my personal trainer, an hour and a half of strength-commanding power yoga, a sizzling and sweaty spin class, a cardio-based group fitness class with strength-training intervals, or even gentle yin or restorative yoga—"me time"—I did something, only stopped by hell or high water, or quite literally a heavy snowfall that shut down a major interstate in Cincinnati in January 2015.

When in movement, I'm happy and I'm at peace. I'm able to press a pause button on challenges I might be facing at the time. I feel proud of my hard work and dedication. My mind stops gyrating around my to-do list and I can fully just be there—in the moment—whether it's through back-breaking burpees, an awakening sun salutation or a recovery and rest.

Just a couple months before being slammed with the realization that I needed help with my eating disorder, I checked in with my personal trainer for my

**I couldn't wait for yoga on the beach of Isla de Ramos while on vacation in Puerto Rico in January 2015—a time of severely controlled dieting and extensive working out.**

monthly weigh in, body mass index (BMI) measurement, body fat percentage check, and measurements of my pectorals, biceps, abdominals, hips, quadriceps and calf muscles. When my trainer revealed my weights and measurements, the numbers had me on cloud nine!

Fitness was an undeniable priority for me. I loved how working out made me feel, and even more, I was obsessed with the physical results that fitness provided. Fitness had given me peace, and it had given me a body that looked like it was carved from marble.

But fitness was also partially responsible for adding something else to my life—something deeper that I'd kept hidden from family and friends, and, at times, I'd kept hidden from myself.

People may have seen muscles on the outside, but they never saw the paralyzing pain and broken soul that were hiding on the inside. **No one ever saw my eating disorder, and no one ever knew I was losing a battle with a crisis that's capable of killing.**

# CHAPTER 3

# Too Type A
# for My Own Good
### *The Pain of "Perfection"*

As my assessment at the EDTC continued, I told Mallory all about the cookie dough disaster that took place just a few nights ago, but not without some tears that I had to wipe away as I remembered the death-defying pain and as I recalled troubles of my past.

I told her that I was too Type A for my own good and that I felt like my personality type had the potential to completely ruin my life. I told her that I see everything as black or white, pass or fail, home run or strike out. I told her that my never-ending need for perfection had bled over into my eating and that I'm unable to find a healthy *medium* (literally) between "good" food and "bad" food.

Countless times I've stopped in my tracks, scrunched up my face and wondered—where did this Type A tendency come from, anyway?

Sure, when I was a child I'd organize my Breyer horse collection by size, my school desk had a particular place for books, binders, pencils and glue, and even as a 1st grader, I'd redo my long, straight ponytail what seemed like 10 times before I was satisfied.

The trend of striving for perfection and winning all the things continued through grade school. Trust me when I say if anyone was going to receive recognition for achievement and take home the coveted certificate to prove it, it was me.

One of the most memorable moments took place when I finished elementary school in 1993. My close friend Deanna and I were chosen to receive special recognition for academic and literary excellence and to recite a poem together as part of the promotion ceremony. We shared feelings of exhilaration and we both had the jitters before taking the stage, but we knew our lines front and back!

Earlier in the school year, something so simple yet packed with power happened when Deanna and I were casually chatting with friends in the gymnasium at a school event. Deanna was discussing whatever we all talked about as 5th graders, and she tripped over one of her words. There she was—the girl who I always saw as so perfect, effortlessly popular, and who I felt so lucky to have become friends with—stumbling over her speech during a casual conversation. And then the next thing blew my mind: Deanna exaggerated the word flop by purposely repeating the mistake and making fun of herself. And guess what? She

Deanna (Mullins) Jewell (left) and I with said coveted certificates at our 5th grade promotion ceremony in 1993 at Deep Springs Elementary School in Lexington, Kentucky.

remained just as cool and popular as ever. From that moment on, even now, I still do the thing that Deanna did: I turn an accidental word stumble into a multiple-word botch and then giggle. From Deanna, I got a good dose of understanding that I can be worthy of friends without being perfect.

As a young Type A, I craved competition. I grew up on a very quiet street with a landscaped median and a court at the east end known as the "keyhole" because the grass was literally in the shape of a keyhole. There were no sidewalks or street lamps, just well-maintained yards and the median between the narrow road. There were 17 homes, five of which included families with children. I grew up a tomboy, playing outside with Paul, Laura, Michael, Hannah, Chris, Chase, Ben and Jackson. Our small neighborhood had quite the crew!

Growing up in the 1980s and 90s, we played whichever sport was in season, rode our bikes, jumped on my trampoline and swam in Chris and Chase's pool. Summers were priceless. We had fun from sun up to sun down, except for when our parents called us in for dinner. During playtime, no matter what we were up to (trouble, I'd bet), I'd somehow turn it into a game, a race or a contest. We couldn't just ride bikes around the keyhole; someone (me) had to win. We couldn't just play with Lego toys; someone (me) had to build the biggest fortress.

One summer morning, Paul, Laura, Michael and I decided to pretend we were going sailing on a ship. We raided our parents' garages for fishing and boating gear, kitchens for food to "live off of" during our days at sea and even our yards for worms we'd use to catch fish.

Somewhere during packing for our sailing trip, I got mad at Paul and went home, pouting like the brat that I was good at being ... all because Paul found something for the sailing excursion that was better than my contribution. With fists fully clinched, I stomped home to find my mom and dad outside and told them about the ship supplies mishap. Still fuming because Paul's stock was swankier than mine, I spotted my dad's paddle—a real, wooden paddle that my fishing-obsessed father used every weekend. Because I got what I wanted in my perfect, only-child world, of course my dad lent me the paddle.

With nothing other than myself, my paddle and my pride, I sat across the street from Paul and the "ship." I gathered my sass and my lungpower and yelled, "Hey, Paul, look what I have for myyyyy boat!"

(I had no boat, only my parents' front patio steps.) Astonished by the real deal paddle, Paul ran over to me and picked up the oar like it was the Vince Lombardi trophy or the Stanley Cup. OK there, I have the best sailing tool, so only now may we all continue having fun.

Fast forward to the present day, not a damn thing's changed. Although I don't have to keep up with the Joneses, drive the newest car, or wear the most expensive clothes or prance around in red-bottomed shoes, I don't stop until I feel as worthy and victorious as the folks in my community, my colleagues and even my friends—sorry in advance, guys.

And really … when I think deeply.… I long to simply be as happy as they are.

While being super competitive isn't the most ideal characteristic, *Huffington Post* associate editor Kyli Singh says a Type A personality drives you "to be the best version of yourself" … insert sigh of relief and "thank you" to Kyli here: _____.

But then again, will we ever reach our "best" selves? Until we can touch the sky or stumble upon some magical miracle … chances are slim to none.

Perfectionists cannot wrap our heads around what "good enough" looks like or feels like. Perfectionists' goals are not quantifiable, so we keep trying and trying to get better and become more efficient, and while we might make progress, we're not satisfied with whatever progress we make, because we always see room for improvement. We never see "good enough." The goal of perfection is unrealistic, and the chase for unrealistic goals can only mean exhaustion, self-doubt and much of the time, misery. We keep running around a track that has no finish line.

I'm sure my perfectionist personality's intense nature leads others to become frustrated with me, as they don't understand how deep the anxiety runs. It's not something that can simply be turned off. I wouldn't even know where to find the off switch.

Others view perfectionists as uptight, rigid, high maintenance, needy, anal … while perfectionists say they just want to be like others— easy-going, relaxed, simplistic and go with the flow. You might feel like others are mad at you often, and you can easily walk on eggshells to ease the misunderstanding. It's a struggle that is made easier with support, patience and love.

Belief: It's not OK to not be perfect because a lack in perfection means something is wrong with me, I could be better, I'm not good enough, and I don't deserve to be happy yet.

Belief: I'm sad when things fall below 100 percent because that means I did not meet expectations and I failed.

Belief: It's not OK to have acne and scars, it's not OK to have thin hair, and it's not OK to gain weight because I feel ugly and unacceptable.

Belief: It's not OK to not complete my to-do list, it's not OK for my house to get messy or become disorganized, it's not OK to forget something when I go on a trip, it's not OK for my life to get off schedule because if this happens, then it means I failed.

Belief: I must work to make all these things flawless because if they're less than perfect, something important will be forgotten.

Really, perfectionists say they just want to be accepted. And perfectionists want to accept themselves. Perfectionists want to feel loved. And perfectionists long to love themselves.

⁓

I gave Mallory details about being overtaken by loneliness on occasion while living in different cities and furthering my career, and I told her that the feelings of loneliness had been particularly severe that year, 2017. Dating didn't really happen. Support was scarce. Friends were few and far between. At some points, my friends were my yoga mat, new clothes, cleaning supplies, my couch cushions, candles, face scrubs and television show characters. My BFF, though, was food. Those things were enjoying my time and company; the people who truly mattered were not.

I spent a lot of time waiting for a silent phone to ring and all I could do was look in the mirror and inside my heart, and wonder what was so terribly wrong with me. I wanted so badly to gain awareness of my flaws so that I could fix them, and so people would want me around. On that summer day in Mallory 's office, I said that if I didn't wake up the next day, I felt like no one would care deeply and maybe no one would even notice for a while. I reassured Mallory that I wasn't currently considering suicide because I was too afraid to carry through with it and didn't realistically have a desire to die. And I guess I had just enough hope left in my broken heart.

I did open up to Mallory about the closest I'd ever come to harming myself: once in summer 2009, I'd taken enough over-the-counter pain medication to keep me asleep for more than 48 hours. I'd take the sedative painkiller and go to sleep. If I woke up, I'd take another dose. I can't remember how many doses I took, but it was enough to raise one hell of a red flag. On a couple other occasions over the years, I'd considered starving myself so that my life would wither away. I hit a really low depression point in April of 2017, and I felt like repeating the forced sleep and starvation. Fortunately, the job I started in January kept that behavior from happening.

As I told Mallory, I heavily connected lonely feelings to my experience living in Cincinnati. It's a very conservative city. It's a lot smaller than Chicago and Atlanta, and I wasn't used to such close networks. It's an "everyone knows everyone" kind of town. Social circles are very small and noticeably exclusive. If a relationship failed in Chicago or Atlanta, the chance of running into that person is slim to none. But not in Cincy … and I'm not used to that.

Cincinnati is that town that typically, when you're asked where you went to school, they're not talking about college; they're referring to high school. High school friendships continue into adulthood, and high school sweethearts are married with kids in short order. If you're not from Cincinnati, it's very hard to fit in, to find your tribe and to have solid relationships. Transplants are kept on the outside looking in—and at arm's length away. People already have established cliques, friends and networks, and so they don't need the new kid. In Cincinnati, it's like the demographic of a 30-something, single, career-focused young professional who values work/life balance is so tiny that it's basically nonexistent. Or at least I almost never found it. I found food, instead.

For the most part, especially when I was younger and was living in cities with greater diversity, I never struggled to find friends, build relationships and secure a support system. But in Cincinnati, I was certainly put to the test. And I'm here to say: I must have it all wrong here. They might call Cincinnati the Queen City … but it has been the king of exclusivity, rejection and pain.

The rest of the discussion with Mallory covered details of my fitness competition training, patterns of food addiction and cognitive behaviors related to eating. Mallory's kind, down-to-earth nature allowed me to feel—for the very first time—content with being helpless.

From there, the EDTC team determined my treatment plan would be the Intensive Outpatient program, the staff coordinated it with my health insurance to ensure coverage, and within just a week my first appointment was in the books.

On July 24, 2017, I arrived for day one of eating disorder camp. It felt like the first day of school. My heart was packed with wonder, uncertainty and hope, and as I pulled open the office door, I knew there was no turning back.

# CHAPTER 4

# Day One
## *Monday, July 24*

*Author's note: I sincerely respect all peers who were a part of the Intensive Outpatient treatment program at the time I was a patient. All patient names have been changed to protect their privacy.*

"Are you Holly?" the receptionist asked. Politely, I confirmed that sure enough, I was Holly.

A sign-in sheet sat before me on the front desk. I wrote the time, 2:30 p.m. EDT, next to the line where "HOLLY PEN" was typed, about halfway down the row of 20–25 names, give or take. For fear of someone knowing who I was and putting two and two together, I asked the receptionist to black out the first three letters of my last name, leaving only "HOLLY" visible on the sign-in sheet.

"This might seem silly," I prefaced, "but just in case."

She used a Sharpie to get the job done and explained that the abbreviated last name, which was assigned to every patient in the same manner, was done to protect patients' privacy under the Health Insurance Portability Accountability Act of 1996 (HIPPA).

I took my seat in the waiting room, a small room with typical doctor's office-esque pale green and yellow leather chairs and sofas, and also an artificial fireplace built into the wall, which, I have to admit, added quite a relaxing touch to the not-so-relaxing EDTC. Shortly after sitting down and soaking in my surroundings, I was greeted by the nurse, Taryn. Taryn led me back to a lab, where my height and weight (once again the numbers were kept secret from me) were taken, and then we proceeded with some standard intake questions … most of which

I'd never been asked before and it was difficult to hold back my sarcasm.

I shouldn't have passed judgment on the intake questions, for some patients may have answered "yes" to some, if not all, of the 10 "Have you ever..." questions that included self-harm and obsessive thoughts, desires and actions.

At this point, I felt very comfortable and optimistic, realizing that I was very fortunate to have answered "no" to Taryn's questions. I felt sincere concern for anyone facing scary struggles, and with all my heart, hoped the EDTC's program would help them find a peaceful, happier place in life. After all, everyone is equal and everyone deserves joy. Once we finished intake, Taryn took me back to the waiting room, where I remained until Mike, the EDTC's practice manager, took me back to his office.

It was hot in there. Coming from someone who tends to be on the chilly side ... it was hot. As Mike read through the orientation materials, I began yawning and tried to seem engaged in what he was saying. I nodded often and occasionally raised my eyebrows in acknowledgment.

When orientation with Mike wrapped up, it was time for yet another waiting period in the lobby. Upon registration that day, the receptionist had asked me to complete a pre-therapy survey. Since I work for an institution that provides education based on research, I happily agreed to take the survey. The time was about 4 p.m., and I had an hour until the EDTC's treatment program officially kicked off.

The receptionist handed me a tablet, which had the online survey pulled up.... ALL NINE parts of the survey. I heard my exaggerated (and accidental) sigh, and pretended to cough so she couldn't detect my annoyance. That's when my patience started to head south. The tablet (not an iPad) was terribly outdated. The keys barely worked. You had to hover the mouse EXACTLY over the tiny circle to select your answer, and as with many long surveys, the questions started to repeat themselves.

I wanted to chuck that tablet across the room and smash it against the bamboo wall where the EDTC entry sign was placed. *Invest in an iPad, people, this thing is a disastrous nightmare!* Finally, after I became disgusted and irritable, the nine-part survey came to an end. As the time grew closer to 5 p.m., patients began coming through the EDTC's doors. I assumed they were part of my Intensive Outpatient group therapy program, but I lacked knowledge to make a fair call.

One girl walked through the EDTC door, quickly signed in and headed toward the door to the back office (where treatment rooms, offices, restrooms and the cafeteria are). We made eye contact and I smiled, but my friendly gesture was far from being returned.

Dressed in Adidas sneakers, black leggings and an oversized gray hoodie, she looked upset and her eyes appeared as though she'd been crying or she'd gone for days without sleep.

A few more girls arrived one after another to the EDTC and sat down in the waiting room, spaced out around me. In a friendly manner, I nodded to each of them whenever eye contact was made. And as it had happened with the first young woman, my attempt at a friendly approach went nowhere. It was awkward and uncomfortable. They ignored me and laughed among themselves with no filters on many of the remarks, including a reference (and an inside joke, apparently) to dry humping.

*Where am I? Am I in the right place?*

I barely tolerated the five minutes I had to sit in the same room with these young women, and was saved when an EDTC therapist, Catherine, opened the door to the back offices and called for everyone to follow her.

Catherine took our group into a large gathering room decked out with rows of connected leather seats that faced each other in a rectangular shape, balloons floating around the room and a variety of artwork on the walls, placed in no particular order. It felt like a classroom for adults—not a conference room, but an average attempt at creating a comfortable, cheerful group treatment space.

Sure enough—there I was—with about 10 other people who, just like me, needed help. I didn't know their stories, their struggles or what exactly brought them to the EDTC, but they were there for the same reason I was—to eventually live a healthier life (or so I thought).

They appeared younger than me by anywhere from an estimated five to 15 years. Each and every patient was dressed very casually, and some looked like they had just rolled out of bed. I found myself sitting in the least comfortable plastic seat as it felt like the cleanest place to sit for the group session. I got the same grossed-out feeling that I used to experience while sitting on a seat on the Chicago L … and already couldn't wait to toss my clothes into the "dirty basket" inside my laundry room. It was like my clothes had become contaminated.

"My name is Holly Pennebaker and I have an eating disorder" was a sentence that I'd mentally and emotionally prepared to announce, but we didn't go there. It was worse. It was deeper.

Each patient took a turn reading their check-in reports, which in a structured manner assessed how they were feeling that Monday. When it was your turn, you'd share your mood, anxiety and irritability levels on a scale of 1 to 10, that you're willing and open to learn rather than learning from the treatment, whether or not you'd "slipped up" with your eating, whether you'd attempted or thought about suicide or self-harm, and what therapies you'd used to help yourself since the last session.

My first day at therapy didn't provide the history that would answer some of the check-in questions, but when my turn came around, I shared what I'd recorded. There was the "My name is Holly" part, and then, on a scale of 1 to 10, I ranked my anxiety as a 7, irritability as an 8 and mood as a 4. *That damn survey and that piece-of-shit tablet.*

Some patients had "good" reports; some had "bad" reports (meaning some were feeling well, and others were feeling sick or upset). As to be expected in a recovery program, sometimes you have happier days and sometimes days aren't so great. I was eager to learn what each patient had to share, partially to see how I compared to them from an anxiety, mood and eating perspective. Was I an outlier? Did I fit in? Did I even belong?

I sat in the uncomfortable chair, and I sat up very straight and tall, poised and proper. Others relaxed, kicked off their summer sandals and laid comfortably on sofas, others Indian-style in large, padded chairs, but everyone looked like they'd made themselves at home. I felt as far from home as I could get.

I sat facing the windows, thinking the view of the neighboring Cincinnati shopping centers would be more pleasant than the views around the room (and offer more sights to help keep my wandering focus occupied).

My eyes danced across the room, still taking in my surroundings: the open discussion area with terribly matched furniture, artwork that resembled something a child would have scribbled with crayons and run home from school to show to Mom and Dad, a sink and counter top (not quite a kitchen), and a tall work table that sat up to 10 people. The slight smell of a hospital lingered in the air, the lighting was a bit dim for a large room, and low-pitched grumbles created the sound of a rushing ocean.

"Gucci…. I hate that word," a petite blonde said under her breath. I then caught her smirking at my large brown leather Gucci handbag, then carrying the smirk and sharp gaze to me.

Completely thrown off guard, I shot my gaze back out the window, so thankful I'd chosen to sit where I could find a "safe place" to go when things got uncomfortable. Using my foot, I nudged my bag closer. In attempt to make a good first impression, I decided to keep my mouth shut.

Monday evening's exercise started just a moment after the Gucci bag hatred took place. A handout came to each of us, and we learned we'd be drawing trees. Each part of the tree represented our life, quite literally, from the ground up.

At the bottom of the tree are **the roots**, which represent where you come from. What values were you born with and what important lessons did you learn growing up?

As early as I can remember, an uphill battle to be the best plagued my every move. The fight for straight A's, to always make the team, to be the most popular kid, to only bring home blue ribbons, gold medals and first-place trophies … no matter how big or small, I had to give it my all, and I had to win. That drive came with a will to lead others, to maintain independence, be in constant pursuit of goals and never stop being the champion.

**The ground** that holds the roots moves into the present day and represents the most prevalent influences in your daily life.

A reflection of my roots, my ground includes a highly competitive nature, talent, skills and knowledge, but on the other hand, that's not enough—it stretches beyond just *having* them.

I crave being needed—that my talent, skills and knowledge are desired by others because I'm able to help make a difference. And I want to be able to do it all by myself too.

I hold onto a soul-shaking fear of failure, fear of regret and fear of making mistakes. If there's room for fault or improvement in my talent, skills and knowledge, that means they might not be good enough for

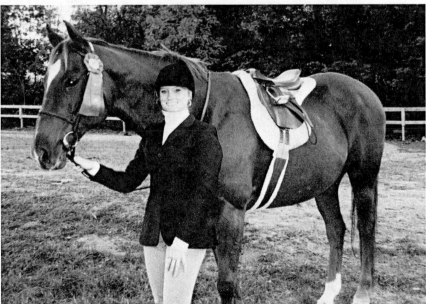

*Top and above:* No matter what age I was, winning first place and getting the blue ribbon was everything, as seen in 1998 and in 2001.

others. And if that would ever be the case, then they'd definitely not be good enough for me. As you can imagine, I've been disappointed in myself more times than I can count.

From the ground, **the trunk** grows tall. Linked to the influences held in the ground, the trunk represents your unique skills and abilities—the things you're really proud of.

*I'm proud to say* that I'm well-rounded. I'm skilled in multiple professions, I've lived in a handful of states and I've experienced many different cultures. I've spent my life riding out significant, life-changing ups and downs and I'm here to tell. I've been exposed to things that can scar someone for life, and while I keep emotional bandages nearby, I won't hesitate to say they've made me strong. Very strong.

*I'm proud* of my athleticism and my physical health. I can compete in most sports and know the rules and plays of the game. The gratitude that I have for my physical health cannot fit into the pages of this book. I have no physical ailments. I can see, hear, smell, taste and touch. I get by from day to day without physical struggle and, to me, that's one of the biggest blessings someone can ask for.

*I'm proud to say* that I'm responsible and reliable, faithful and loyal to people and commitments. If I tell you I'll be there, that I'll handle a project, and that you can count on me, I will make sure I follow through with my word. I will never lie, cheat, steal or do harm to anyone. I will treat others to the best of my ability. I will fight through the thick and thin of a relationship so that the bond remains unbroken.

From the trunk come **the branches**, which hold your hopes, dreams and aspirations.

What BIG goals, if you accomplished them in your lifetime, would make your life complete and bring you the ultimate sense of accomplishment, success and explosion of joy? Perhaps your branches are a efficacious career, unconditional love shared with family and friends, top-notch health and freedom from injury and ailment—the sky's the limit. No matter how unique, as long as they matter to you more than anything, those visions make up your branches.

From the branches grow **the leaves**. The leaves are important because they represent the important people in our lives.

Think of whom you turn to for love, companionship, support, guidance and enjoyment.

My leaves include my family, my best friends Pamela, Alisha, Jamie, Libby and Amy, my mentor, editor and friend Mike, my former executive editor and current mentor Michael, my former boss-turned-friend Kathryn, and sometimes, my inner self. And dogs. And puppies.

The people who are there—no matter what—to lift you up when needed, who have resiliently ridden through good times and bad, who've helped you get to where you are today and who can be relied on for their open hearts and open minds—the people who move you to be the best person you can be—those are your leaves.

The leaves of your tree bear **the fruit**. The fruit represents any gifts the important people in your life have given you.

These gifts are the best types of gifts—the ones you can't see, touch or hold. They're felt by only your mind, soul and heart.

What have you received from each leaf that's helped you to grow and prosper? Perhaps you wouldn't be where you are today without their gifts of encouragement, feedback and criticism, and support, without their holding you accountable, without their exemplary examples to follow, without their love and shared laughter.

Anything you'd like to thank your leaves for—those things are your fruit.

Now, you have a complete tree. It's important to know that your tree—your life—will be weathered, tested and sometimes destroyed by storms, and so **the storms** represent anything that might be a threat to your life.

What could hold you back from making your dreams a reality? What could keep you from optimal, authentic happiness?

Worries might come in the form of financial resources, time constraints, distractions that disrupt your commitments, lack of self-confidence, family trouble, health and even death.

Take a moment and think about how you'd handle these threats—how you'd rise above the storms.

If and when a crisis hits your tree, animals might come along during the storm, and the animals are the important people who you can call on for help—who can get you back on your feet once the crisis fades. These people must be strong in times of calamity and be able to handle emergencies.

If you're like me, your animals might match the people listed as your leaves. The same people who add the most precious value to your life are those who add cherished, special care and encouragement without judgment. They openly help without expecting anything in return, and they guide you through the storm with their very best will, never once leaving your side. And, of course, without judgment, you'd do the same for them.

---

The clock struck 6:15 p.m. and dinner was announced.

A pounding in my heart returned and picked up pace, but the walk to the cafeteria felt like walking through applesauce. It was a slow, single-file march and I had to force one foot in front of the other as my anxiety worked to push me back down the hall, to the plastic chair that faced the windows. For some reason, that chair instantly became my safety net.

*WHOA. I'm walking single-file down a hall, steps away from having an organized, supervised meal.* My stomach turned. My anxiety took flight. I started smelling the mystery dinner, and a particular flashback from when I was a young child commanded my every thought.

A 4-year-old, I was at a Lexington, Kentucky, daycare. I remember learning my ABCs, making crafts and coloring with crayons, the excitement of playtime and … the daycare deal breaker: lunch. Placed before me at daycare was a plate of food, and on that plate was something that made my skin crawl: green beans. I ate the other food, and one of the faculty members told me to eat the green beans and, as expected, I didn't want to. And so I didn't. The teacher got rather commanding and, as a little girl, I became scared and started to cry.

*Not the green beans! I don't like them! They taste yucky! No! I won't do it! They'll hurt me! I'll die if I eat them! They're so gross! I won't live if I eat the green beans!*

The crying turned into a temper tantrum—the type of thunderstorm that I can remember very distinctly some 30 years later. It was so bad that my mom had to come early to pick me up and take me home. That was the last day I spent at that daycare. It would be private babysitters for me from there on out.

As I entered the EDTC cafeteria, I found myself in the middle of the line, about halfway from the front and so halfway from the back. As I got closer to the selections, all hope of having an enjoyable meal was crushed. The first food I saw was a mixture of cooked peas and corn floating in hot water, some sort of tofu skewers (for the vegetarians in the group), cheesy au gratin potatoes and cuts of beef that were soaking in what looked like an au jus. I didn't want anything to do with any of it.

The vegetables were a hard stop—no shot, no chance of those things getting anywhere near my plate. The potatoes were actually appetizing, but my hesitation rose from the acne and inflammation that would be caused by the cheese. I didn't want the meat, but at least it was some protein, which would satisfy the strength-maintaining part of my meal.

I ate the potatoes fairly quickly. A food I rarely eat, the cheesy potatoes tasted very good. I could have had a second serving, but assuming that wouldn't be allowed, I didn't even ask.

The meat was terrible. It was cold, dry, and it tasted like mounds of salt had been pounded into every bite. During several bites, I drank a sip of water just so I'd be able to swallow a bit easier. With about half a piece of meat remaining, I was done. I didn't want to fight it anymore—the challenge of chewing and swallowing that came with each bite. It didn't taste good at all and finishing the meat wasn't worth the work.

A staff member had sat next to me at dinner, and I was thankful for her company as I labeled her as "normal" compared to the peers in my group (another form of judgment I wish I could erase). When she saw me fold my napkin and lay it across my plate, she very tenderly told me she'd have to give me a "boost."

"Like the brand name Boost? The supplement drink?" I asked.

The nutrition supplement was a product I'd never considered consuming for my own nutrition needs, as I thought it was made for young children and elderly people.

Yes—that's the Boost she was referring to. The nutritious shake thing that I only hoped tasted better than chocolate chalk.

The EDTC staff member actually offered a non-dairy version. I think I shocked her by being so willing to drink the supplement. After all, I wanted all the protein, vitamins and nutrients I could get. In the same, familiar manner used when I drank a pre-workout supplement before hitting the gym, I chugged the entire cup full of thick, fruit punch-flavored juice. Not bad at all!

I soon learned that the goodness of Boost products is no joke. Mike Reilley, who edited my first couple drafts of this book (and is an afore-mentioned leaf), said that Boost drinks are to thank for keeping his father, Bill, alive for weeks beyond what doctors expected. The nutrition supplement helps maintain healthy blood sugar levels in elderly patients. Mike said toward the end of his father's time, he'd feed Mr. Reilley Boost drinks through a straw.

Thirty minutes after dinnertime began, our time was up and we went back to the treatment room for "Meal Process," which is a time to reflect on the meal we'd just eaten … or choked down … or refused to touch.

I picked up my pace on the way back so I could be sure to snag the same "safe" chair from before. The majority of Processes as described by my peers were that the meal felt OK to eat and didn't cause too much fret, but no one seemed overly thrilled either.

When a few seconds of silence came after the last person took their turn to Process, I offered to share my thoughts, as long as I was told fully what "Process" meant.

Catherine was surprised and welcomed my input. It felt like authentic encouragement, which at that point of frustration and doubt felt awesome.

I let the group and group leaders know that I hated the meal. I wasn't satisfied. I didn't get full. I was barely able to swallow the cold, dry, sodium-packed meat, and I was borderline craving something sweet to balance out the salt.

I kept quiet about the fact that I had a mango/chia seed fruit bar in my purse, and I considered coming up with a plan to eat it. *Do I sneak off to the bathroom, bag in hand? Should I lie and say I'm on my period and that's why I need to take my bag to the restroom?*

Get a grip, I told myself. It was too early in the game, and I didn't want to act out in a way that I'd regret, especially on the very first day.

I used Process to talk about being non-content. I openly admitted that I felt like I might be wasting my time and questioned if I was sup-posed to be there. *Am I in bad enough shape for this?* I wasn't comfortable, and I certainly didn't expect the group's warm reaction, which rushed straight to my overly-guarded soul.

The support and all its might busted out the gates, to the point that telling the story didn't do it justice. Everyone's face suddenly glowed, everyone's attention was suddenly undivided, and everyone's body language became so incredibly open.

"When I first got here, I thought these people were sick. Just stick with it," said Harper, the girl I saw in the lobby with the oversized gray hoodie who looked very disturbed and despite her petite body kind of (in a gentle way) frightened me, just a little.

Harper's face turned sweet and her disposition became incredibly genuine. She's a beautiful young girl. She has an unforgettable smile and a very positive glow about her.

"If you think you're not supposed to be here, then that means you likely are," another girl said to me from across the room. I noticed her steady eye contact and the slight wrinkling of her forehead when she talked. It was clear she meant what she said.

"I wouldn't have gotten this far in treatment without these people in this group," said Joyce, the third girl to pass encouragement my way.

There was a special softness about Joyce. While her face showed worry, I could tell that her thoughts came from a place of kindness and it was evident she really cared about this new path I was taking with treatment and seeking recovery.

Then, the strangest thing happened: everyone started snapping their fingers, repeatedly, with both hands.

"Now, what's all this snapping mean?" I asked with a slight giggle. I was starting to realize there was an EDTC lingo and some practices I'd have to catch onto.

Snapping is EDTC's version of a clap.

**So there I was, applauded on my very first day, by a group of strangers who had just become my support system ... all in a *snap*. A *judgment-free snap*.**

Harper spoke next for Process and shared her clashing considerations in trying to decide whether to break up with her boyfriend before moving to Chicago for her freshman year at Columbia College.

Between the initial connection I felt to Harper and now her soon-to-be Chicago residence, I was immediately emotionally invested in her.

Since I'd lived in Chicago for six years, and a big piece of my heart will certainly always be there, I wanted to help Harper because I know first-hand how amazing the Midwestern city can be. I wanted to hold her hand. Of course she didn't know this, but in my mind I gained a new little sister in Harper.

"Oh!" I reacted out of delight and excitement for the new journey on which she'd soon embark.

As for the boyfriend, he seemed to be leading source of Harper's stress, and so I suggested that Harper have a real conversation with him.

"Maybe you and your boyfriend should have a chat about expectations, and make sure that your expectations for each other and for the relationship are in alignment," I said. "If you both are on the same page, then perhaps no one will get hurt in the end."

Harper was very receptive and her eyes lit up as if she'd finally found the light at the end of the tunnel. Even Catherine gave me approval and said she liked my advice. Harper thanked me, and for her closing thought (as everyone shared that evening), she said she had serious conversations to have with a few people over the next week, including herself.

My closing thought for Monday, July 24, 2017: **Embrace vulnerability and opportunities to feel uneasy**. The only person who cares whether you *look like* you've got your shit (life) together is you.

# CHAPTER 5

# Day Two

## *Wednesday, July 26*

Day Two wasn't set to take place until Wednesday evening (the next regularly scheduled time of treatment), according to the original plan. However, I unexpectedly returned to the EDTC first thing at 9 a.m., thanks to an impromptu meeting with my dietician, Isabella.

Isabella and I had exchanged email messages Tuesday, which made me realize that this whole "dietician chit chat" needed to happen sooner rather than later ... because I *know* how to eat healthy and how dare someone tell me otherwise, right? *Check that ego and go sit down, Holly.*

Refusing to think that my strict, self-made diet is wrong, no matter what a dietician tells me, I'd written to Isabella on Tuesday.

*I don't believe my work toward recovery complicates the meals, but instead, my preferences and likes/dislikes. I'm an extremely picky eater and always have been. That's not going to change. My mother had to hire a private sitter when I was growing up, who would prepare meals to my liking. Daycare attempts didn't work because the staff wanted me to eat foods I didn't like. Even as a very young child, I wasn't having it. I was picky and I still am.*

*Last night's dinner, for example:*

- I don't like cooked peas or corn. I only eat organic, cold, raw vegetables.
- I eat minimal dairy, so the cheesy au gratin potatoes went against that. Plus, I'd avoid a potato that's not organic, for fear that it's been sprayed with harmful chemicals.
- I eat minimal meat: fish and poultry only. If I eat beef (which

was served last night), I make sure it comes from grass-fed cows and that it's clean. I avoid pork altogether.

*When I'm eating in the way that's best for my health, I eat according to my Pitta dosha, per Ayurveda.*

- Clean, organic foods are a must across the board. Artificial additives and chemicals are a hard stop.
- No fried foods that are prepared in heavy oils because they're hard to digest.
- No red meat/no pork.
- No dairy (I allow a minimal amount).
- Nothing spicy/heavily flavored.
- Zero preservatives (which tend to be added to foods that are cooked and prepared in large amounts … like the catered food that's served at the EDTC).

(I even went so far as to suggest bringing in my own prepared meal for Wednesday's dinner. I can only imagine how poorly that idea went over with Isabella. It certainly got shot down when our meeting rolled around.)

Isabella's response:

*I can see that you have put a lot of thought and care into this response and I would like to be able to talk about this further. We strive to recognize individual needs and preferences while also offering education and support about what we know works in addressing the eating disorder.*

The meeting with Isabella was comparable to the majority of first dates I've been on—awkward, invaded by a forced politeness and a disingenuous smile, and when I got to leave, relief that it was over. Only with Isabella, there'd have to be a second date.

Outside of whenever my binge eating spiked, I'd exclusively eaten organic foods as part of a clean diet for years, but yet with that very meeting, I had someone telling me that a recovery center—a resource for eating disorder help that promotes healthy eating habits nonetheless—sure enough would refuse to serve organic meals.

And where, exactly, does an EDTC dietician get off disregarding my belief and faith in Ayurveda—a science that began *thousands* of years before modern medicine, and has become one of the world's most sophisticated and powerful mind-body health systems of the present day?

Ayurveda "offers a body of wisdom designed to help people stay vibrant and healthy while realizing their full human potential," according to Deepak Chopra, M.D., a world-renowned pioneer in integrative medicine and personal transformation, who's also board certified in internal medicine, endocrinology and metabolism. Chopra is a fellow of the American College of Physicians, a clinical professor at UC San Diego School of Medicine, a researcher in neurology and psychiatry at the Massachusetts General Hospital, and a member of the American Association of Clinical Endocrinologists.

To top it off, he had a Twitter following of 3.2 million at the time I began treatment.

How can Isabella's knowledge even begin to compare with that of Deepak Chopra? How dare she not support my preference to eat according to the science of Ayurveda? I don't even think she'd ever heard of Ayurveda, for crying out loud!

For those readers who need an introduction, allow me to fill you in: Ayurveda is a personalized approach to health, dependent on your mind-body type. There are three types: Kapha, Pitta and Vata.

Once you identify your mind-body type, you make optimal choices about diet, exercise and supplements, and all other aspects of your lifestyle with the result of your finest mental clarity, your body functioning to the best of its ability and, perhaps most important, your feeling your very best.

Now, what's EDTC got on *that*?

It made no sense that the EDTC's treatment approach would focus on the treatment group as a whole instead of addressing our individual nutrition needs based on our mind-body identification—something we're born with and that's likely different from that of our neighbor.

I insisted that my mindfulness practice and knowledge of how various foods impact my body put me ahead of the game. My competitive nature fueled my belief that my comprehensions of which foods most fit me and my awareness of how each food made me feel were enough to make me better than the next person.

I was beyond certain that I was right and that Isabella was wrong.

I judged Isabella's well-researched guidance and didn't even give her a fair shot at helping me, a fair shot that she definitely deserved.

I totally discounted her professional level, experience and knowledge in the dietetics field. Only later would I discover that the guidance Isabella provided would be the only instruction capable of making a difference, and also capable of making me change. **At that time, my ego blocked my ability to trust Isabella.** Without judgment, I should have accepted Isabella's support from the get-go. I should have welcomed her management of my diet with open arms, completely trusting that Isabella only wanted what was best for me.

*But my smoothie is clean! But my smoothie is raw! Don't tell me that my smoothie isn't the most perfect smoothie ever!*

I left Isabella's office that morning with my smoothie of perfection in hand, a sizeable chip on my shoulder, and one hell of a judgment-based attitude problem weighing on my heart.

When I returned at 5 p.m. for my second-ever treatment at the EDTC, I still felt incredibly conflicted from my morning meeting, and that's exactly how I showed up. I was irritated. I was confused because my healthy choices that I'd made for as long as I can remember were actually seen as unhealthy choices by an eating disorder specialist.

I knew I wasn't going to get my way—a pill that's incredibly hard to swallow for an only child with more of a Type A personality than one soul should ever have.

My attitude was shot.

Plus, patients are supposed to sign in and out whenever they come or go, and I realized that I hadn't signed out after my morning appointment with Isabella.

*They better not scold me for this.*

I was ready to fight.

In the waiting room, a young woman with deep brunette hair and wearing a blue T-shirt and cropped jeans was sitting on the sofa where I'd begun sitting, so I chose the seat next to her. She appeared quite composed and cleaner, more put-together than Monday's bunch, so I secretly elected her my new friend.

I asked to borrow her phone charger and she was very eager to share, which told me she was cool, easy-going and good-natured. We exchanged names, and I felt fairly comfortable around Sophia.

A few minutes passed and the EDTC doors opened. To my surprise, the rest of the patients arrived Wednesday with a different energy than they brought Monday. The vibe seemed brighter, livelier, a whole new world of cheer and laughter. It lifted my spirits and I reminded myself of the **mantra** I'd practiced since Monday: *I will look forward.*

This mantra does not mean "I'll look forward to what's next" in anticipation that the future holds something good, bad, or anywhere in between. Instead, by saying *"I will look forward,"* I empower myself and allow myself to strip judgment from my views of tomorrow, the next hour, even the next minute. No matter what might come, *I will look forward* free of judgment and with no expectations. *I will look forward* with a judgment-free mind, ready to accept whatever's next, no matter what. If I look forward, I know that I'll be able to handle anything, mishaps and miracles, and that once I get through them, I'll be more empathetic and aware, stronger and better than before.

I exchanged half-smiles with a few familiar faces, and shortly it was time to head into the treatment area and get started.

I was one of the last patients to check in Wednesday after some frightening, really low mood scores of 1s and 2s. My spirit sank upon hearing how bad my peers felt, but my heart felt hope for Joyce, who reported a mood score of 1. She'd been so supportive of me during my first night, and I wanted her to be happy. She cracked a joke and laughed twice within the next 15 minutes (so hopefully, surely, her mood wasn't actually the lowest score possible).

Once everyone had made their mood, irritability and anxiety scores known, our Wednesday evening therapist, Kennedy, left the room for just a few minutes.

When she returned, she carried two objects—one in each hand—to be used for the evening activity. When she marched with determination and a stern expression into the middle of our circle, you could have heard the gasps a mile away.

Two scales stood before us, one black and one white, one analog and one digital, both the same size and square shape. The look on every patient's face showed terror, hate, and resentment, but no words came from anyone.

The main portion of this exercise required each person to share how the arrival of the scales made them feel. My group had some serious revulsion when it came to these two items. It was like the scales had the power to grow legs, gain might and viciously attack everyone at the EDTC that evening.

We were given about five minutes to write down observations, note reactions and jot down any details we'd experienced and we'd like to share regarding the scales. Trying to think outside the box and come up with thoughts different from the group, I jotted down the scales' function and goal.

*Using either a digital display or a moving needle, each scale served the purpose of reporting a measurement.*

*The scales' goal: to accurately weigh an object and to supply that measurement to the user.*

When it came time to share, I spoke of the scales' job and objective. I also questioned how reliable the scales really were. Could their report be trusted? What if the scales were off?

In connection to the fear instilled by the scales when my peers first laid eyes on them, I also pointed out our assumption that the scales were indeed meant to measure a human.

What if the scales were to be used to measure something else—an animal, a package, or another object?

If you take away the cognitive connection between scales and human weight, they're not so scary anymore. Think of the scale as a device used to report the measurement, in pounds and ounces, of SOMETHING, instead of automatically seeing the scale as a device that's going to judge you and report that judgment in the form of numbers, to further decipher how "good" you are. **You're perfect, and the scale has no right to weigh in (literally) on your worth.**

I shared my non-reaction to the scales, saying that I'd never really worried about the number that shows up. I hadn't owned a scale in years, and the last knowledge I had of my weight was several months before when my personal trainer evaluated my progress in the last month I'd trained with him (March 2017).

Because I could tell this was a highly sensitive subject for many of my peers, I tried to speak from an objective place and to remove any arrogance from my tone. I truly didn't feel better than anyone because scales didn't bother me. I wanted others to realize that they should never obsess over a number or let a number define how good of a person they are.

Wednesday evening's exercise was an outlet for some deeply ridden emotions and troubling stories I hadn't expected to hear. They were too concerning to seem possible.

One of my peers (who will remain anonymous in this case) said that on Tuesday, her father told her to get off her lazy ass and walk the dog. She said she asked him politely to be sensitive of her condition, told him that his remark had hurt her feelings, and that her recovery was nearly impossible with harsh comments like his. She said the conversation grew

**Using a resistance band for a strengthening exercise during a personal training session in March 2017.**

heated and he began yelling at her, saying he was tired of walking on eggshells around his own daughter, and that he couldn't take not knowing how to communicate with her any longer, so long as she was being treated for mental health illness.

By now, tears were streaming down my peer's face and a few nearby group members held her while she finished her story. Her father's hurtful words pushed my peer over the edge, and she (once again) threatened to kill herself, all while consumed by panic and fear—fear that she'd never be good enough, fear that she'd never have the relationship with her father she so desired, and fear that she'd never find healing and peace.

She craved his understanding, to be treated like a caring father should treat his daughter. All she wanted was love.

As if an alarm had sounded, my peer was showered with genuine support, some of which shot down her father but was meant to keep her spirits up, help her move on from the argument and to bring her some reassuring light. I sat there frozen. I wanted to give my peer the unconditional love her father wouldn't provide, but I was unable to react, in utter disbelief of the story I'd just heard and the emotion that had erupted in the small room.

She was able to soak in love from the comfort her EDTC friends provided her, and we ended on a positive note: a dear peer's heart refilled with hope.

The activity and story took up time until dinner, and so started the single-file line to the cafeteria.

The food smelled a bit better than the first night's spread. I was eager to see if my talk with Isabella would make things better this time around, and sure enough, there was one small change that totally made my day. Instead of my only fruit/vegetable option being the cooked, processed food I refused to eat, I learned that a raw apple had been set aside just for me! Bonus—it was a Granny Smith apple, my favorite!

I skipped over the vegetarian dish that didn't apply to me, and saw one of my favorite foods of all—mashed potatoes. They certainly weren't prepared to my preference, but I couldn't wait to dive in. I asked the meal supervisor how much I should "plate" (like, plate used as a verb), which equaled about two scoops. There were small piles of melted butter here and there, so I aimed my scoops for the back corner of the pan, as far away from the butter pools as I could get.

"Or … you could mix them," the supervisor hinted.

I shoved her words in one ear and out the other and I kept my mouth shut, although I was having a shouting, judgment-filled explosion on the inside, as if that would be a substantial barrier between my plate and the butter.

*Screw you! No, I'm not going to mix in the butter. What you don't know is that I've had twenty corrective procedures on my face for acne scars, to revise a skin problem highly attributed to dairy consumption.*

*How many surgeries have you had? How many years has your life been tainted by painful, paralyzing acne? I'll scoop the potatoes that are farthest away from butter and you can leave me the hell alone.*

I'm sure my lack of poker face said everything out loud, and from there I moved on to the meat portion of Wednesday night's meal.

Generally speaking, if I don't love a certain food, the portion I eat will be on the small side. Wednesday's recommended serving of pork was three medallions. I expressed that I wanted to take only two, but apparently that wasn't going to fly.

"At least put it on your plate," the supervisor said.

"But it will just get thrown in the garbage and I hate to waste food," I fired back, thinking of Cincinnati's homeless population and the fact that there was at least one hungry person within a block that would love the EDTC's leftovers. The supervisor wasn't convinced.

Feeling my "throw a fit" limit not too far off, I flopped three pieces of pork onto my plate and then took my seat.

I cut the slimy, fatty outsides from each medallion and as I intended, ate two of three pieces. The mashed potatoes were gone in 60 seconds, and the apple's core was the only remaining part of the fruit.

I was a little more satisfied and relieved too—my stomach had started to growl with notable volume before dinner.

But lo and behold, the dinner didn't end without me chugging my Boost in the kitchen—all thanks to that one piece of pork, that against my will, was tossed in the trash.

I was aggravated and felt a hint of anger, too, because two of my peers were served an Amy's Kitchen frozen *ORGANIC* meal of vegetable lasagna. *Had I not just requested organic food that same morning in Isabella's office?*

By the end of the second treatment session, I was sure that this EDTC camp wasn't for me. I was positive that I could make healthier options on my own without the help of a center that wouldn't support my preferences, once again, based on deep knowledge of how my body handles various foods.

Process passed very quickly Wednesday night, but I paid very little attention to what was being shared until we reached the session's dismissal. Instead, I was weighing other options, considering where else I could turn for eating disorder help. A regimen designated to outwardly express feelings about *a meal* wouldn't fly for a weeks-long treatment plan.

I was two steps from being out the door when something happened that damn near set me off: I "got in trouble" for drinking tea.

I brought in my Yogi brand tea from home, but in a reused disposable cup from an area coffee shop.

An EDTC staff member introduced herself, and I did the same with a handshake. I was then told that according to EDTC policy, no outside beverages were allowed in, and that I was limited to water kept inside a clear container.

OK … maybe I didn't get scolded or penalized, but I'd done something that was outside of EDTC policy, so in my mind, it felt like I was being punished.

"TEA!?"

My eyes displayed shocking disbelief, and wrinkles of confusion and frustration crossed my raised forehead.

Buckle up. Here we go again…

*Screw you! What you don't know is that there's a carefully-planned reason for me bringing the tea. It contains kava, one of the trendiest wellness ingredients out right now. It promotes stress relief so it makes perfect sense to sip on it during a stressful session, and I don't want to drink it too close to bedtime because I don't want to be woken up multiple times during the night needing to use the bathroom.*

Sure—it's as simple as don't bring in outside drinks. But what I later learned from this experience is to chill out and listen to the reasoning of others, as their rationale may very well come from a very good, trustworthy place, and I should be fine with "their way" rather than mine.

I operate in a way that comes from extreme independence and strict self-governance. Every move I make, everything I do, every choice I elect is carefully thought out, deeply analyzed, and I weigh all possible good and bad outcomes. I don't allow myself to become the squirrel in the middle of a busy intersection because each decision I make comes with unparalleled strategy. Everything must accomplish something, or at least make an effort to do so.

And I'm far from being right. And in no way do I know it all. (On the inside, I'd actually known this for a long time.)

I brought that realization home with me Wednesday night. I've never wanted to fathom, let alone accept, that others know what's best for me because that meant sacrificing control of my actions and decisions, and in the end, not being prepared for or knowing the outcome.

**Control had become an unbreakable safety net, or so I'd thought. And little did I know, just a couple more treatments would start to change that.**

The EDTC's talk of the importance of social support systems drove me to drop my plans for the night and call a couple of my close girlfriends.

When I reference "plans" for the night, I should clarify that those plans meant writing this book and finishing house chores. **Fun still seemed like too far a stretch. Fun seemed unsafe.**

**I visited Amy (left) in November 2015, before the severity of my anxiety had set in. We had a blast tailgating and attending the Pittsburgh Steelers home game at Heinz Field.**

My friends Amy and Libby both answered my calls, and despite my hesitation, I revealed that sure enough, I was about a week deep in eating disorder camp. Amy lives about five hours from Cincinnati in Pittsburgh. Since our friendship began in 2013, we've discovered a long list of things we have in common (even our middle names), and we're able to share anything and everything with each other.

Libby's apartment is just about 10 minutes away from my place, in the nearby Walnut Hills neighborhood.

I'd been consistently noncommittal to plans with Libby, and it hurt knowing I'd let her down multiple times within that last month or so. When I told her what I'd been going through, two and two came together real quick: I couldn't commit to plans because I never knew how I would feel when the time came to hang out. Likely, my anxiety and depression would keep me from going out in public, afraid that my shame would be enhanced and that my comfort level would be jeopardized. **Isolation had seemed like the best option. Isolation felt within reach. Isolation felt safe.**

Of course, Libby offered undeniably genuine support and told me to call her ANYTIME I needed her. Let me tell you, Libby is the real deal when it comes to friendship. She's the friend that when she says she'll be there for you, she means it.

I'll never forget a Thursday evening in the fall of 2015. I'd just finished a yoga class, and it hit me that I HAD to end my then-current relationship with someone I'd been dating for about a year. I called Libby on my drive home, barely able to speak because of the heavy sobs. Seconds after I stepped inside my

**Just weeks after the breakup, I attended a Cincinnati Bengals home game with Libby (left) after I unexpectedly snagged a ticket!**

apartment, Libby was there knocking on my door. She held me (even though I was drenched in smelly sweat from yoga), she forced me to eat a small dinner (which she put together after digging through my fridge), and she wouldn't leave until I was OK and able to smile again.

# CHAPTER 6

# Day Three

*Saturday, July 29*

I woke up with a chip on my shoulder Saturday morning, and brought the chip with me to the EDTC. Opposition became more intense with every Hyde Park block I drove through. People out jogging, folks gathered at the local coffee shops enjoying their time with one another, pet lovers walking their faithful companions, and others driving to their Saturday morning fitness and yoga classes (just like I should have been).

Hyde Park is a vibrant, wealthy neighborhood commonly referred to as the "gem of Cincinnati." With every commute through its streets of old town charm, you're sure to see Hyde Park's residents out and about being active, living their lives that seemingly revolve around health, fitness, hard work, socializing and fun.

As my reluctance took over, I felt resentment build up at the same rapid pace. The thing I wanted to do was taken away by the thing I *had* to do, which meant my body, muscle growth and image satisfaction would suffer.

I pushed through the EDTC doors with zero plans to participate unless called upon, and as childish as it seems, I just wanted to spend the next three hours pouting in a corner with my arms folded tightly across my chest because I didn't get my way when it came to how I spent my Saturday morning.

But a little light of happiness was switched on when Elise, a younger patient in my group, joyously greeted me with a "Hey!" right when I walked in. It was the first time she'd shared any enthusiasm with me, and honestly, the earnest and friendly gesture felt really good. I felt like, at the very least, someone had chosen to say hello. It was just enough to turn my frown upside down and for me pass the friendly gesture on to the next person.

I'd become so isolated during that time in my life that I felt lucky to receive a warm greeting from anyone at all. In fact, I cannot count the number of nights that when I laid down to go to sleep, I thought, if I were to not wake up tomorrow, I doubt many people would even notice that I'm gone.

I replied to Elise's hello, expressing gratitude for her welcome.

I still whined and moaned about missing yoga Saturday morning during check-in, but my regret and complaining were soon broken up by two celebrations: Joyce and another peer, Alice, were completing their programs, and Saturday marked the last day of their Intensive Outpatient treatment.

Two EDTC staff members, Kennedy and Phoebe, called on "Words of Wisdom" from the group (thoughts from others to send the two champions on their ways). A couple peers shared memories, encouraging pieces of advice and cheer for the girls and their accomplishments.

Though I'd only known her for just a short while, Joyce left a lasting impression on me and I couldn't keep quiet.

*Joyce, I've only exchanged a few words with you during the last two treatment sessions, but I want to share something I've observed about you. On Wednesday night, you said that your mood was a "1" and then minutes later, you opened up to us about a pretty awful argument with your father. I'm so sorry that you went through that rough evening with him. But within the next 15 minutes, you smiled multiple times, you laughed multiple times and you made others laugh multiple times. I thought ... if Joyce's mood is really a "1" ... girl.... I just don't know. You bring a special energy to this group and you have one hell of a spirit. No matter what circumstances go down outside of you, never let those dim your light. I can tell you're ready to shine bright!*

Joyce nodded, thanked me, and her ear-to-ear smile reassured me that speaking up was the right thing to do. I can only hope to have helped Joyce realize her beautiful, internal power.

I couldn't leave Alice out—the petite, timid girl who was so soft-spoken that I'd leaned in to hear her during dinner the pervious Wednesday evening. Alice had overheard a conversation in which I mentioned getting my master's degree in journalism from DePaul in 2011, when I was 29 years old.

And so Alice told me she, too, took classes at DePaul for a year.

No way! A fellow Blue Demon was sitting right there at the same dinner table as me. That was something special I had in common with this sweet, soft soul. I told her I went to school in Chicago's Loop and she said her classes were in Lincoln Park, so we'd covered ground on both of DePaul's campuses.

Until that conversation, I'd mistakenly made the assumption that I wouldn't get to know Alice because she simply didn't speak much at all. Her voice was barely audible when she did talk, and she seemed so scared of being heard.

But there was something about Alice that moved me whenever I made eye contact with her. There was a sharpness, intelligence and insight. I felt like mighty competence was stuffed into her small frame. Her eyes showed a passion to make a difference in the world, and with the right amount of confidence, she'd be unstoppable.

I let those observations and hints of spirit guide my Words of Wisdom for Alice on Saturday morning.

*Alice, you're so shy and soft-spoken. And at dinner on Wednesday when you mentioned that you took some college classes at DePaul, I was so happy you'd talked to me. I had to move closer to you to hear what you were saying, and when I look at your eyes, I can tell you have a big, bright essence inside of you that can't wait to light up the world and really make big things happen for yourself and for others. Remember that you're able to do anything your heart tells you to do, so never be afraid to be loud and go big!*

The care for Joyce and Alice that I'd developed over just six or seven hours ended any and all bitterness I had felt Saturday morning due to missing my plans, and the resentment I'd filled my heart with before arriving at the EDTC. Those girls deserved all the glory they were given for their commitment to a better life, the struggles they'd overcome and the positive spirits they'd take into the world. Joyce and Alice did it— they were officially in recovery!

And on that note, it was time for snack. Saturday mornings didn't include a meal, but a snack. I'd heard that snack means you get to select from an assortment of food. Talk about a sigh of relief!

I still took plenty of anxiety to snack time, wondering if there would be anything that I liked, and something that wouldn't trigger a craving since Saturdays are the most difficult days to avoid binge eating.

I was able to breathe a little easier when I saw a banana. I eat a banana just about every day, and I don't mind bananas that aren't organic because of their thick peels. That banana had my name written all over it!

Quickly, while standing in the snack line, I learned from a peer that "Exchange" was the word used for a serving ... lots of new EDTC terminology to learn. For snack, I was supposed to choose two Exchanges. With my trusty banana clinched in my left hand, I scanned the selection to see which item might be the best to complete my snack.

The array of food ranged from several fruit selections, chips and crackers, raisins and dried cranberries, and even Oreos. I could have stood there all day, analyzing each snack option and why each one would or wouldn't be the perfect choice. But I had to choose. The line was moving and we were allowed only 15 minutes to eat. Anxiety used its force to bring my right hand to the box of Craisins. I'd feel fit and pretty if I ate fruit; after all, it was the "safest" option.

Not that it should have surprised me because I couldn't seem to get it right in the food line at any meal so far at the EDTC, but come to find out, my snack wasn't approved because I could only have one fruit Exchange.

Rev up the anxiety engine. It was time to make yet another food choice. Hearing my "hurry up" voice speaking on the inside, I grabbed a bag of pretzels, which seemed like the next-safest food, and I took my seat.

But if something is safe, doesn't that imply a need for protection? **And if we're talking about food here, what could my selection of fruit possibly protect me from?** It would soon all come together.

Sure enough, the light bulb came on later in the weekend. I was driving, as most of my "genius" moments tend to happen during commutes.

JUDGMENT! That's it! That's the reason why the simple task of choosing two items for snack was such a big deal.

According to my own false postulations, the banana said I'm fit, health-conscious, know potassium helps with muscle cramps, and that

I prefer raw (better) food. The pretzels said that I care about my figure because I chose them over the potato chips (junk food) and cookies (also junk food).

*And of course, everyone will think the same thing too. How could I possibly eat Oreos in front of others? They'd think I have the food maturity of a child, and that I don't care about the bad impacts sugar and the artificial ingredients have on my health. They'd think that I'm not as good a yoga instructor because I eat junk. They'd think I'm a hypocrite who talks a big game about fitness but doesn't back it up. They'd think I don't care about the bloat I'd have after eating a serving of Oreos. They'd think that because I'd allowed myself to eat a common, household favorite chocolate cookie with vanilla filling that I, too, am just common and average.*

I'd attached a meaning to what the snack choice said about me, without considering that I cannot in fact prove what others think about me based on my own judgment. Until our thoughts, and even fears, become proven evidence, they're false and fueled by judgment. After all, everyone is innocent until proven guilty.

(Just for the record, Oreos taste better than fruit and pretzels and the "real me" would choose Oreos over fruit and pretzels any day.)

I met with my therapist for the first time after treatment that Saturday, right at noon. Together, we determined three goals for treatment that, if I could achieve them, would bring the joy into my life that I'd been seeking for nearly two decades.

1. Normalize eating habits.
2. Escape black-and-white thinking and comfortably live in the gray area of life.
3. Get "fixed" so that I'm no longer drowned by an eating disorder, anxiety and depression.

With accomplishment of these three goals, I'd live an untroubled life of freedom, happiness and serenity. It meant other people would love me more, and it meant I'd love me more too.

# CHAPTER 7

# Day Four

## *Monday, July 31*

Oh, what a night Monday turned out to be!

I'd made a promise to myself to be open, *completely*, to receive knowledge and feedback from the EDTC staff and from my peers, and trust that it comes from a compassionate place. I'd repeated to myself that if I stayed on my ego-induced high horse, then I would never get anything out of the program and I would never reach recovery.

But Monday turned out to be the day that would suddenly end that promise to myself.

The company I work for changed healthcare insurance providers, which meant costs would change for employees, both on family plans and on individual plans. The context behind this fiasco is one for another day, but the change meant a lower paycheck because more money was needed to pay for the new premium.

Needless to say, I started Monday feeling screwed, especially because I was single and apparently, that had to do with the increase in health insurance costs. (I'd yet to fully understand the reason behind the rate change, and I hadn't realized my company's generous contribution to each employee's healthcare expenses.) I'll end it there—it's a soapbox I don't need to get on in this book.

I was also struggling with a lack of communication at work, and my self-doubt was coming in like a monumental wrecking ball. I knew I couldn't continue the workday feeling so heavy.

The entire day may have been saved with a deeply assuring, constructive meeting I had with my boss late that morning. Within a short 20 minutes, we were back on the same page and I was once again feeling like a professional rock star.

Overwhelmed by what had proven to be "a Monday," I went into the evening's treatment with "get me outta here" written all over my face. That may have been why I nearly jumped (literally) when I joined Elise on the elevator and she told me that I looked pretty. Of course, I felt far from pretty. I worked at a very casual office where jeans on the regular were absolutely part of an acceptable dress code. Our business-causal dress code is often more like a business casual-casual-casual dress code. On that day I wore black jeans, a red and white striped t-shirt and nude ballet flats. My hair was parted down the middle and the lifeless locks just laid there, naturally fine and flat, falling over my shoulders and down my back. My face wore minimal makeup—just enough to conceal my acne scars, highlight my cheekbones, fill in my light eyebrows, and darken my eyelashes. No glam going on whatsoever. **I guess Elise saw something that I simply did not … or maybe that I *could* not.**

I signed in as usual, and at 5 p.m. sharp, the group was back in one of four now-familiar treatment rooms. My anxiety was a 7, my irritability a 6 and my mood, thanks to the world's best boss, was a 9.

Part of the check-in process involves sharing with the group what support they can provide to you on that night of treatment. I let everyone know that I hadn't eaten lunch until about 3 p.m. and that I was dreading dinner, which was just one hour and 30 minutes away. I was full. I was satisfied. I felt good about the salad, yogurt and (not organic) snack crackers I'd had for lunch. The last thing I wanted to do was to stuff food into my packed stomach. I didn't NEED to eat again at 6:30, and more than anything, I didn't WANT to.

*If binge eating is about stuffing yourself to the point of discomfort … why would the EDTC staff ask me to do the same thing—to eat when I'm already full? The hypocrisy was almost too much to handle. I wanted to yell, unleash my anger and throw a classic temper tantrum.*

But I knew I had to find a calm—a level of chill that would carry me through the evening. **"I will look forward. I will look forward. I will look forward." Silently, I repeated the mantra until I became present and one with the group.**

Monday night's exercise was about body language, and we spent about 20 minutes watching a TED Talk from social psychologist Amy Cuddy.

Cuddy, who is particularly interested in body language, theorizes that changing your posture can considerably change the way your life grows and evolves.

Body language is a form of nonverbal communication and inter-action—it holds meaning and it has an impact on others. Your body language can determine who approaches you, whether you get invited to events, and even whether you get a job offer.

Do you tend to hunch over and make yourself smaller? Do you cross your arms? Do you cross your legs and your ankles?

"We make sweeping judgments from body language, and those judgments can predict really meaningful life outcomes," Cuddy says in her talk. "We tend to forget the other audience influenced by our non-verbals and that's ourselves—thoughts, feelings and physiology."

There are nonverbal expressions of power and dominance. It's about opening up so you make yourself big. Expressions of power are global and go back ages.

Think about what your body looks like when you win a race, score the winning basket, get a promotion at work, or win a prestigious award.

According to Cuddy, when you feel powerful you're more apt to BE powerful. So whatever body language makes you feel the most pow-erful—use that in your communication.

And use body language in your fight against your eating disorder. Invite motivation to help yourself be mindful of your body language when you feel triggered by your eating disorder.

Use "power poses," those that make you feel like Wonder Woman or Superman, to fight any fear that comes up when your eating disorder urges surface and to carry you above and beyond unhealthy cravings and temptations.

Your strong presence and powerful body language are mightier than fear, and they can ensure the most successful outcomes when bat-tling an eating disorder.

Before watching the video of Cuddy's talk, my EDTC peers and I partnered for a power pose exercise. Madelyn was my partner, and I was really eager to work with her. Madelyn certainly seemed like some-one I would want to be friends with, someone many people would want to know. She's funny, humble, spontaneous, and she smiles often.

First, we stood facing each other, tall and proud with our hands on our hips, and we carried on a conversation for two minutes.

A sense of simplicity and satisfaction came over me as Madelyn and I talked. We were comfortable standing tall during the short conversation, and we naturally rocked instead of forcing our bodies to stay perfectly still. We kept solid eye contact and exchanged some smiles and laughter. We also leaned into each other, as if showing we wanted to hear more about the other.

Next, Madelyn and I began a new conversation. This time, we crossed our arms and stared at the ground while we talked. It was so difficult for Madelyn and I to speak with each other without making eye contact. We caught ourselves making gestures with our hands and arms, realizing that so much nonverbal communication comes from our eyes and faces. We had no way to smile at each other, no way to express sympathy, no way to see support in each other's eyes and no way to see each other's reactions. There was no exchange of emotion. We were left with tone of voice as the only tool to keep the conversation going.

The exercise took both physical and mental work. In society, we make many fearful assumptions of others, and of ourselves, based on body language and nonverbal cues. However, our assumptions lack necessary evidence of how a person really feels and who he or she really is. It's impossible to KNOW how someone else feels without asking—it's information that only evidence can provide.

I guess you could say that by dinnertime, I'd "worked up an appetite" despite being so full when treatment began, but that would be far too inappropriate to vocalize inside the culture-rich walls of the EDTC, a place where I was *still* learning all the rules.

An unbearable weight was lifted from my shoulders when I walked into the cafeteria that Monday. Mashed potatoes and turkey—now *that*, I can handle. Plus, I was told to skip the cooked, steaming green beans and head for the small fridge where raw, cold carrots awaited me.

So there's something about mashed potatoes. I really like them, and for no reason in particular. Maybe my love for mashed potatoes comes from having had them for dinner fairly often growing up; maybe it's simply the soft texture and hint of salt. Regardless, I had no complaints when mashed potatoes were served at the EDTC. Like usual, they hit the spot. In fact, mashed potatoes may be my favorite side dish.

In my mashed potato bliss (OK, maybe they weren't *that* good), a red flag was abruptly raised inside the EDTC cafeteria.

Susie, the dietician I recognized from the previous Monday, sat down to join Caitlyn, April, Jackie and me. I saw a down-to-earth staff member in Susie for the first time, and I decided to engage in conversation with her, thinking I'd like to get to know her. My iced-over heart found the slightest sign of kindness in Susie. But something on the outside was missing—she had no plate and she had no food.

My eyes shot over to Beatrice and Scarlet. Hmmm … no plates and no food over there, either. No EDTC staff member was eating dinner with us. Instead, they were accompanying us while we ate, their eyes making frequent checks on our plates.

The room temperature must have shot up some 20 to 30 degrees within just a second or two. I was hot. I felt lied to, betrayed and angry that these best practices, as administered by the staff, weren't being practiced by the staff.

*So if this is the perfect meal with the ideal number of Exchanges, ideal balance, ideal amount of nutrients and vitamins … and if 6:30 p.m. is the best time for us to eat … then why aren't you eating the food and why aren't you eating with us? What do you eat and when do you eat it? You have to lead by example. Practice what you preach. I'd feel more comfortable if you were a part of dinner, instead of creating a bigger separation between staff and peers. If you're really supportive, you'll integrate more with the group instead of making yourselves different in a superior way. Are you too good for the food? Are you too good to eat with us?*

Judgment entered the situation at the speed of light, and it kept me from considering that there was likely a very logical reason why the EDTC staff wasn't eating and watching us eat instead. As if right on schedule, I blew off steam the minute Process provided the chance for me to do so.

So what we're providing isn't the "perfect" meal, Scarlet said, because that's not what EDTC's therapists are trying to achieve. We're using exposure therapy to make you feel more comfortable and get closer to nonjudgmental feelings when it comes to food.

Scarlet's spider analogy explained it quite well.

Let's say you're terrified, with a severe and incapacitating fear of spiders. In order to get over your fear of spiders, you'd very slowly expose yourself to spiders in regular sessions of exposure.

At the beginning, you're at one end of a room and at the other end of the room is a spider (your fear food), sealed inside a jar. Notice your anxiety, avoidance and changes in behavior caused by the spider.

At the next session, you'd move just one step closer toward the spider. How would your anxiety, avoidance and behavior feel then? You can't run away from the spider. You have to experience being present with the spider.

Maybe the next session comes the next day and maybe it comes the next week, but when you arrive at the session, you move another step closer toward the spider.

And in the next session, you take another step closer toward the spider.

You get the drift. Over the course of time and repeated exposure, you take steps that inch you closer toward the jar with the spider inside.

Once you can tolerate being near the jar, it's time to take off the lid. Now, the spider is capable of touching you. You've been exposed to the worst possible scenario when it comes to your fear of spiders.

And you're here. And it's OK. You discover that the spider won't hurt you and that you're able to be present with the spider and carry on as usual while being exposed to the spider.

You learn that although you were terrified of what you believed certain foods might do to your body, because of repeated exposure, you're no longer afraid of those foods.

You've exposed yourself to those foods and eaten them on enough occasions over time that they're now common, and you're no longer bothered by them. Plus, your desire for "safe foods" has significantly decreased, or it's no longer a F.E.A.R.–based practice.

The food is selected to meet nutritional requirements, but it's not selected based on what you see as "safe foods." We're not going to serve you meals that are comfortable for you to eat, Scarlet said. We're going to push you out of your comfort zone so you see food in a new way, with no meanings or judgments attached to the food.

**All food fits.** That's our philosophy, Scarlet said. It's not supposed to help you reach your highest level of health. It's supposed to make you feel more comfortable with the "spider."

At first, confusion consumed every reaction I could have mustered. I thought my goal for the end of treatment was to achieve optimal health and finish treatment in a healthier place than where I started.

But that's NOT the EDTC's goal! And there you have it—I was wrong! Right there in that very moment I realized that I didn't have it all figured out and that I was way out in left field. I'm actually wrong! **It felt surprisingly good to be wrong, too, probably because it exposed me to a new place of actualization and relief—it was OK to be wrong.**

What a bright light Monday night brought to me on the way home (yes, back in the car and right on par with the cognitive magic that happens there).

The light rays exposed me to a thought—a thought that was so profoundly powerful that I wanted to scream my fresh perspective from the top of the highest mountain and then throw a pop-up dance party.

*As long as I eat safe foods (foods that don't cause guilt or worry), I won't grow and I won't break old, false habits. My dieting is F.E.A.R.–based = False Evidence Appearing Real. My F.E.A.R.–based perceptions of food had mapped out my diet for so long, I was fully committed to believing false evidence of the way various foods would affect me.*

*What a relief it would be to actually not care about organic restrictions, "clean" eating, raw food consumption and avoidance of my laundry list of "dangerous" foods! The joy and freedom of choosing what to eat without heavy, infinite analysis, judgment, or worry about what others would think sounded like the new best place on Earth. In some ways, like the freedom to choose, cost and availability of food, I'd be at an advantage because my body handles nonorganic foods just fine. I'm in a better place because I don't have to hold on to the stress of worrying about every little thing I put in my body and what it might do to me. I can just eat and enjoy what I eat. I can have my cake and eat it too. Freely.*

# CHAPTER 8

# Day Five
### *Wednesday, August 2*

Now that I've survived three days of treatment, I want to remind my readers (and myself) that this book was never meant to be a memoir. Instead, it was to be a place where the lessons I learned while living my life could be shared, and if I'm truly living out my passion, then your life may be better because you allowed my story to be a part of it.

At its core, this book's mission is to provide information that empowers, inspires and motivates others, and even makes others' lives better, more peaceful and enjoyable by leaving a lasting, memorable impression.

It's about helping people to overcome fears; to discover freedom and live their best lives possible—an opportunity to make holistic happiness and transformation accessible through a success story that was only possible after I got help.

To anyone reading: have compassion for yourself and others on all days, good and bad. Be proud of every single fear you've overcome, every single achievement you've made along the way, and your experiences and knowledge gained along your own unique journey. Love yourself and others unconditionally.

Do I have the credentials of a professional therapist or dietician? No. But I do have a powerful story to share, in real-time when it happened, and I've acquired a wealth of knowledge from professionals that I believe will benefit other people.

The fourth day of treatment began with a discussion about social media, and if you're like me, you have a love-hate relationship with it. At its worst, social media is the epitome of inauthenticity, an outlet for people to paint a glorious picture, share an opinion (welcomed or not), and tailor their stories to tell a story they *think* people want to hear.

It's like social media adds testosterone to real life—it pumps up, energizes and adds volume to what is actually an authentic life. Social media is a way of turning Professor Sherman Klump into Buddy Love, displaying a character you *think* people will (literally) "like."

A Facebook post might show photos from someone's marvelous, magical vacation in a tropical paradise beyond your wildest dreams. But chances are, you're much less likely to find a post about someone's run-of-the-mill trip to the grocery store, in which the highlight was finding yogurt on sale.

The good stuff I find in social media is being able to see how distant friends are generally doing, reconnect with important people from your past, and even make new friends. I met one of my close buds on Twitter, and it's a very authentic, down-to-earth relationship. We might not hear from each other for weeks, even months, sometimes, but we pick right back up, and it's always a pleasure to hear from Matt.

Social media is also a great way to support a cause you care about, develop a business and bring people together for an upcoming event.

No matter your feelings on the pros and cons of social media, there are snippets of truth in all platforms. We discussed Wednesday that social media creates challenges for many people every day. Someone with an eating disorder can be super-sensitive to messages that images, lifestyles and stories give off. There's infinite information to be shared and consumed, and we often find ourselves caught between what's credible and what's not.

Content can be altered by image-perfecting tools like Photoshop, filters and apps like Whitagram and Facetune; the truth can be stretched and blurred; and your own interpretation can be skewed depending on how you ingest what you see. Does her body really look like that? If I eat such-and-such foods, and avoid such-and-such foods, will my body really notice that much difference? If I take the advice I see on social media, will it really transform my looks and my life (even just bits and pieces)?

Some social media messages resonate well with people, but others can bring harmful impacts to someone with an eating disorder. When a social media message commands people to do something, change something or take action in some way, the message works in the same way an eating disorder works. The disorder commands people to believe a notion—it's a voice inside their heads that talks loudly about food and eating, and it can straight up paralyze people's ability to think clearly.

Wednesday night's exercise put me in close touch with those commands. My eating disorder tells me:

- "I'll never be free from attachment I have with various foods."
- "I must be judicious with food, and I'll always over-analyze what I eat."
- "There's always going to be an unidentified hole that I need food to fill."

In response, I say:

- "You're right. I'll never be able to eat and *actually just eat.*"
- "You're right. I'll never be able to stop examining and scrutinizing food."
- "You're right. I'm lacking something in life, and instead of finding happiness through that unknown satisfaction that's available somewhere within myself, I'll resort to food instead."

**I've listened to my eating disorder for a really long time, and I've allowed it to create my reality.**

Notably, I'd taken a baby step into my new eating philosophy earlier on Wednesday, around lunchtime at work. I'd packed a salad and a half sandwich: one slice of organic honey wheat bread, organic mixed greens, organic turkey, vegan-friendly cheese and a small dab of honey mustard. To top off my plate, though, I allowed myself to have (ahem … *enjoy*) a snack-sized pouch of Ritz cheese crackers … and all the non-organic shit that came with it.

It was a little thing, but it was a big move toward the gray area that I've never, not once, never ever found comfort being in. That goes for food, life and all the above.

Living in the gray area means separating judgment from my thoughts and getting rid of my black-and-white thinking. It means looking forward to what might come instead of preparing for the unknown. It means making decisions more readily. It means … wait for it … wait for it … challenging the belief and the "rule" that the perfect thing exists. *I will look forward. Perfection does not exist. I will look forward.*

# CHAPTER 9

# Day Six

## *Saturday, August 5*

My alarm blared at the strategically-set time of 7:12 Saturday morning ... yes, I have the amount of time I take to get ready and get out the door down to a science, which allowed plenty of time to pack an overnight bag for a little weekend getaway. Saturday morning's treatment at the EDTC started at 9 a.m., and packing didn't take quite as long as I'd planned for, so I found extra time to delete some emails and get in a little book writing.

I opened up my email to find a message from a New York City–based wellness blog that I subscribe to, which sends out a monthly energy horoscope. I don't really drink the Kool-Aid when it comes to these forecasts, but with each sentence I read, the energy report became more spot-on with the shit I was carrying around.

According to the horoscope's writer—television host, speaker and spiritual healer Alyson Charles, better and internationally known as RockStar Shaman—August was the month to think BIG as we take on healing of traumas.

For those who don't know, RockStar Shaman says she ran into an enormous spiritual awakening years ago when unexpected trauma hit her life hard enough to bring her to her knees, but, at the same time, led her to better align with her calling as a shaman. As a shaman, she provides "sacred knowledge" and "divine energy" to others, and she's able to powerfully promote and facilitate positive change.

I was so engulfed by the August energy horoscope that I read it about three times, pausing to connect each part with where I authentically stood in that Saturday morning moment.

*What is also opening up is a new way of looking at things—one that is filled with much less judgment (of self and others), which will open your heart center more and allow you to have a higher and broader viewpoint in terms of what you are capable of being, doing and experiencing in this lifetime.*

*The theme for August is initiation, for it's when we allow ourselves to know ourselves in full (light and dark) that we can begin to embody our complete power; the deep, ancient wisdoms in our soul spark once again to life. As the false self fades and we merge more with heart and soul, we get clearer and clearer on what truly feels right to do here on Earth.*

*The other key for August is finding the gold within the disturbances, the miracle within the difficulty or pain. This month can present scenarios that may appear dark, but this is where the work begins—being able to pivot your lens and perspective over to the flow of wisdom that will also be there, and showing you the magic, fortune and enrichment that lies within areas that might feel troubling.*

Did ya hear that? "This is where the work begins!" "Enrichment that lies within the areas that might feel troubling!" I was blown away by how closely the energy horoscope matched my story, and the struggles and goals I was facing moments just before my sixth day of eating disorder therapy.

The 20 minutes it took me to read and digest RockStar Shaman's forecast were all I needed to set the tone for Saturday at the EDTC: **A new perspective, less judgment, an open heart and seeking wonder when things get hard—on and off the court.**

I decided August would be THE month, more than any other month of 2017, which I would take the initiative in making big change happen.

Transformation out of black-and-white thinking, as I'd come to realize in the most hardcore way, would be the prime path to dissolving and eventually taking away my constant anxiety.

Within the last few treatments, I had become so very clear on how very terrified of a gray area I really was.

If you think of stepping the tip of your toe into a pool of cold water … well, let's just say I'm still on the deck looking at the water from afar, clutching the safety of a black-and-white float. The water looks so clear, invigorating, pleasant and delightful. The ultimate feel-good place on a hot, sweet summer day.

But the swimming pool's water seems so "risky and dangerous" that you sit on the deck, scorched by the sun, crushed by unanswered desire, and beat down by your inability to submerse yourself in the refreshing, nice-and-cool place of enjoyment.

Starting early August, no matter what, I'd inch myself into the awesome swimming pool … even if it meant I'd need a raft to help keep me afloat. There might be times when I'd feel like I was drowning, but my determination to live in the gray area would be the force that would keep me above water.

Saturday's session at the EDTC was the most educational one yet, from which I learned some solid strategies to take with me along my first sets of practices steps into the gray area of life. Out of black-and-white thinking, and into the wild gray wonder!

The EDTC uses **dialectical behavior therapy (DBT),** a healing method that teaches patients that two different things can exist at the same time. Black-and-white thinkers find it very difficult to believe that both things are true.

For example, let's say you wake up in the morning feeling unrested, stressed out and grumpy, but you also know you've got an important day of work coming up and another commitment when your workday ends.

By using DBT, you'd say out loud, "I'm in a bad mood, AND I'm going to have a great meeting with my boss." You would not say, "I'm in a bad mood, BUT I'm going to have a great meeting with my boss." The word "but" negates the ability to TRULY have a great meeting. The practice of DBT helps black-and-white thinkers believe that despite feeling irritable, the meeting can and will be great.

As a binge eater, I'd use DBT to say:

- "I'm craving pizza, AND I'll be satisfied with one or two slices."
- "I may have eaten a bit too much during that meal, AND I don't feel guilty."
- "I really want to eat a cheat meal tonight, and it's cool if I eat a balanced dinner."

Another therapeutic practice the EDTC uses in treatment programs is **urge surfing**. Urge surfing is an exercise in which you sit with urges instead of immediately acting on them and try to get past them. Urge surfing helps people develop a tolerance for triggering thoughts. The practice allows you to realize the impulse is *only* a thought, and you have the choice whether to act on it. The impulse cannot control you.

When black-and-white thinkers feel a really strong urge, it's extremely difficult not to react because perfectionists are easily super-activated. Black-and-white thinkers want to satisfy or fix the urge instead of accepting the urge and living with it. It's like we want to ride on the surfboard, but we don't want any waves to come—big fans of a no-wake zone.

A binge eater could practice urge surfing by saying, "I had a challenging meal and I am a binger. I have a lot of judgments about what I just ate. I can and will sit with it and realize I have an option and I have a choice."

Given the option of sitting with the urge or reacting with anger and emotion, urge surfing, when practiced over time, will bring patients a sense of calm by helping them learn that the urge WILL stop eventually. Biologically, you cannot operate with that much anger for a long time, according to EDTC therapists. The time you must sit with the urge is determined by its intensity … maybe 15 minutes, maybe more. No matter how long you have to ride out the wave, the craving WILL pass. You must trust that the craving is only temporary.

The next strategy taught by the EDTC reminded me of meditation, what Headspace CEO Sean Brecker says has the power to cause normalized mind health in an increasingly fast-paced, overwhelming world. The EDTC simply calls it **grounding and mindfulness**.

You can try it yourself by first sitting in a chair with your hands resting beside your hips or thighs, and your eyes either closed or focused on an empty spot on a wall in front of you.

"Let me feel my feet on the ground. Let me feel my ankles below my knees and the stretch of my pants over my knees. Let me feel the texture of the chair underneath my palms. Let me feel my shoulders relaxed above my hips. Let me feel my head above my shoulders and my chin either parallel to the ground or very slightly tucked. Let me feel my breath move through my body at a slow pace, allowing my lungs to fully expand and fully let go."

Next, tell yourself where you are, literally. This really makes sense—

think about it: you can't think about your brother's brother's brother in Oklahoma if you're fully focused on, and present with, the texture of the chair underneath your hands.

You can't think about how badly you want the most perfect pizza if you're fully focused on four-count inhales and exhales of breath moving all the way from the tips of your toes to the crown of your head, and back down again.

"My mind is only on this moment. I am not going to react. I'm going to sit with my emotions until they settle down, and I will no longer want to engage in eating disorder behaviors. I am going to allow myself to worry for five minutes, and then check back in and focus on the mind work I'm doing and that I'm proud of."

I'm going to be here now (literally name the space where you are located at that moment).

Grounding and mindfulness is ideal to relieve the struggles of perfectionism and allow oneself to actually, like, *really*, chill out. It helps the black-and-white thinker give up control without giving up hope and happiness.

The EDTC teaches patients to practice **distraction**. When an initiator causes you to be angry, distraction is a therapeutic, actionable exercise that takes your mind and focus away from the source of anger— the thing that pissed you off.

Distraction might mean getting up and leaving the room. According to the EDTC, distraction means going somewhere else—somewhere you can change your mindset and you won't be susceptible to urges and anger.

When you put yourself in different surroundings, you're more likely to take your thoughts away from the stimulant that suddenly changed your energy and activated worrisome emotions.

You might distract yourself by directing your mental energy toward something you enjoy. Think about moving away from something frustrating to geeking out over your favorite TV shows, games and DIY projects.

Chances are, hobbies and chores will be good distractions to refocus your effort and energy.

Try distraction by saying, "This situation brings me pain and discomfort, so instead of holding onto anger, I am going to concentrate on a simple, short-term goal. By committing to and fully focusing on this activity, I'll let go of the anxiety I feel right now."

The final therapy covered in the EDTC's program is **cognitive defusion.** I asked for clarity during Saturday's session at the EDTC. "Defusion" is the term they use instead of diffusion as I thought at first!

Cognitive defusion is a means to create separation between your thoughts when you're triggered and thoughts when you're *not* triggered. Black-and-white thinkers find the separation very hard to achieve because they hold their beliefs strongly—they're attached (aka *fused*) to their ideas. Black-and-white thinkers are very confident that their triggered thoughts are true and that they represent reality. If achieved, separation by cognitive defusion allows them to realize the falsehood of their thoughts and detach from the exceptionally strong bond that has been created in their minds. Cognitive defusion shines light on the actual reality, which is a place free of attached meanings, judgment and fear—it represents the truth.

Cognitive defusion takes the thought from the person's mind and puts it out in front so he or she can take a look at it. Someone with an eating disorder might say, "When I'm in my binge-eating mindset, I'm not myself because I'm fused to ideas associated with my eating disorder instead of my real self."

The F.E.A.R.–based thought comes before a fact-check that allows someone with an eating disorder to distinguish between fact and fiction.

"I'm having the thought that I'll only be satisfied after eating a whole large pizza because eating only a slice or two won't fill me up— it won't be enough. Plus, if I eat pizza, it will count as a cheat meal and I'll fail in my clean-eating plan, and if I'm going to fail, I might as well go big or go home."

Fact check: "The reality is that all food fits. The reality is that I can eat a slice or two of pizza without feeling any guilt. The reality is that I can sit with the serving of pizza and be OK with it. Clean eating and short-term diet plans are false because I *can* experience freedom and non-judgment with food. The tempting desire to eat the whole pizza is false because there's no such thing as failure with food."

## CHAPTER 10

# Day Seven

### *Monday, August 7*

Not a good night. Not a good night at all.

I wanted to be at home, away from the EDTC and the stress I felt when under that roof. I'd spent Saturday away at a lake in northern Kentucky with my mom and some friends, and then Sunday in my hometown. I was excited about the opportunity the day at the lake provided—to practice some gray-area eating and living. There were endless snacks readily available throughout the day along with plenty of beer and margaritas, and a huge, home-cooked roast beef dinner was waiting for our crew when we got off the water that evening.

I kept my grazing within reason and I didn't have any binge-eating episodes, but I definitely crept into a very uncomfortable place with food by the end of the weekend.

*Had I eaten the "right" amount of food? Had I made the best selections? Had my anxiety been so high while exposed to so much food that I was on the brink of a binge?*

I had to make so many food choices over just two days' time, including where to have lunch while out with my mom on Sunday in Lexington. We went to a new pizza restaurant, where we shared a mixed green salad and a margherita pizza. The meal didn't trigger any eating disorder behaviors, but it did give me enough anxiety to stretch into the evening. For dinner, my family and I ate out, and I ate a small burger and a serving of fries … true story: I ordered from the kids' menu. And I'm not 12 years of age or under.

Because I ate pizza for lunch and since pizza is "bad," my all-or-nothing mentality told me a "bad" burger and fries made the perfect dinner for that Sunday.

The guilt, worry and regret that followed made it all too clear that I was nowhere near recovery, and I was so mad at myself for letting those burdens and F.E.A.R.–based thoughts back in after such a strong week.

When it came time for Monday night's session at the EDTC, I was still holding onto judgment and remorse from Sunday and I let it be known that I felt like I'd backtracked into some of my old beliefs and behaviors. **I felt the judgmental black-and-white thinker inside me once again take control of my story ... and take control of my life.**

*Could I really not just have a fun day on the lake and a stress-free hometown visit? Did it all have to be haunted by an eating disorder?*

I wanted to do what was so familiar—go on a crash diet for three days eating only raw foods (when I'd sometimes feel close to fainting), drinking at least a gallon of water and pulling two-a-days at the gym. A crash diet—the strategy my friends and I would execute the month before college spring break vacations—had always been the quickest route to regaining confidence and feeling comfortable with my body. If I'd eaten a bit too much "bad" food, a short time of extremely restricted food consumption would take me back to a "good" place with my body and self-esteem. It would take me from black to white (or white to black), and I had to get there as fast as possible, so that I spent as little time in the gray area as possible. I couldn't be somewhat happy with my body. I had to be 100 percent happy. Not 98 percent. Not 99 percent.

Monday's exercise was anything but "appetizing." It sounded lame, and just to be straight up, I didn't want to do it. I didn't even want to be at the EDTC that night, let alone engage in some self-affirmation exercise. I wanted to work out so that I could "make up" for damage done over the weekend. I wanted to be at home, unpacking my weekend bag and setting myself up for a good night's sleep. I also wanted to eat ... or should I say drink ... a protein shake that would help take my body to the feeling of what a "fit" girl's body "should" feel like.

But I wasn't in any of those places Monday evening. I was in a treatment room, in a Cincinnati office building, looking out over the streets below.

*I will look forward. I will look forward.*

*Get present, Holly. You're here because you're sick and you need help to get better. Trust the EDTC professionals and have faith in the effectiveness of the exercises. You have to be here. Put in the effort. Do the work. Your recovery is depending on it.*

**I will look forward. I will look forward.**

I felt my mindset shift, and even if it was the slightest glimpse of hope, I felt a new sense of commitment to Monday's exercise. We began self-affirmation work—writing down our positive qualities in the areas of the physical, emotional, intellectual and social. The assignment was easier to complete than I thought it would be.

**Physical:** Pretty eyes, naturally blonde and straight hair, strong body and in good physical health, athletic ability

**Social:** *Are you kidding me? I'd lost more friends in the last couple years than I had lost throughout my entire life. I felt pathetic, terrified of the "nobody likes me" notion that had consumed my every (failed) effort of getting out and about, and actually enjoying having fun again. Fun had become a memory, a pastime, and in no way, shape or form part of my current life. There were a considerable, and quite frankly, scary number of nights that ended with me lying in bed, covered with cotton sheets and sadness, wondering if I didn't wake up the next day, would anyone even notice? Would anyone care?*

*Dig deep, Holly, dig deep. You have a lot to offer. Dig it out of your kind, loving soul. You MUST.*

**Social:** I include everyone so no one feels left out, I take chances by thinking outside the box, I'm a fairly free spirit, I'm not afraid to do things alone, and I've never met a stranger.

**Intellectual:** Well-rounded, knowledgeable, mindful, helpful, insightful—I'm good at finding a unique angle.

**Emotional:** Loyal, reliable, passionate, detailed, deep-thinker, willing to love but terrified of being hurt.

The point of the self-affirmation work was to realize that each of us have a good number of things we like about ourselves, and that we also have the strength to recognize them and present a few to the group.

Plus, if the positive qualities can be acknowledged in the present, then that means they can be seen and utilized in the future, when those with an eating disorder get down on themselves.

Let's once again revisit the unrealistic beauty ideals and the pressure they bring to someone with an eating disorder. How can the ideals and standards be resisted, minimalized, or better yet, avoided altogether?

There must be some sure-bet strategies to fight off unrealistic beauty ideal promotion and exposure.

As you can imagine, that was the second part of Monday's exercise: body activism.

My list of ways to battle the negative impact of unrealistic beauty ideals:

1. Avoid Facebook and Instagram (I'd gone eight months without them as of mid–August 2017)
2. Stop social comparison
3. Work to become less competitive
4. Use a normal mirror to apply makeup (I use a mirror that magnetizes my face 10 times that of a normal reflection)
5. Stop body checking: looking in the mirror, touching parts of my body where I feel less confident

Body activism success is dependent on actual implementation. You must do what you say you're going to do and make it happen in a public sphere: the part of social life where people freely identify and talk about societal problems. Implementation requires adaptation to a different attitude, one that allows you to create an agenda in your mind and follow that agenda according to how it was laid out, with an intention, so that you can make transformation possible.

The EDTC therapists recommend following through with one body activism plan per week. They say that with one executed plan per week, you can change key attitudes and behaviors so that you're able to align with more positive thinking. By engaging in one body activism plan, you'll give yourself the opportunity to challenge society-ingrained, unrealistic beauty ideals, and step by step, week by week, you'll shift into positive feelings about yourself. You can learn to love yourself by letting go of the baggage of unrealistic beauty ideals and the pressure that comes with them.

Well, there you have it folks … the lame exercise became the reason I was suddenly in a better mood with lifted spirits … just in time for dinner.

My taste buds and appetite jumped for joy as I walked to the cafeteria, the smell of Italian food dancing through the air, getting down with its bad self.

And then I saw it—a big, fresh, gorgeously green salad and chicken penne Alfredo. It was about to go down with the same call to celebration that came with the NFL Super Bowl Championship and the final game of the NCAA Basketball Tournament.

I loaded my plate with as much salad as I thought I could get away with, then arrived at a choice between Italian or ranch salad dressing. You might need to regain your composure after I say this, but I've never cared for ranch dressing. It tastes like a metallic, sour, sharp, poor excuse for something to enhance the experience of eating a salad … and all the other stuff you people drown with ranch. So I reached for the bottle of Italian dressing, and I was told to stop, that the ranch had been documented in my meal plan for that night.

"But it's a taste preference problem for me. I've never liked ranch and I never will. I'm not eating it. I'd rather have my salad dry."

The EDTC dietician went on to tell me that they'd have to give me a Boost nutritional drink for refusing the ranch dressing.

"But there's zero nutritional value in ranch dressing!" I shot back.

*How can you possibly compare a nutritional supplement drink to a spoonful or two of the worst condiment on Earth?*

I was getting hot. I could feel the burning in my face. My breathing deepened and my chest tightened as if it was a washcloth being wrung out.

The dietician reminded me that it's not about the nutrition; that it's about being OK with eating whatever is served.

"Put me down for a refusal, or whatever standard operating procedure applies to my decision," I said. "I'm not eating ranch because I don't like it. I'm not drinking the nutritional drink because it makes my stomach hurt."

From there, I found my seat. I felt my body temperature and my temper slowly cool down as I enjoyed the delightful Italian dish and choked down dry salad sans dressing.

After dinner, it was once again time for Process, and once again time to openly react to dinner. I hated to throw another temper tantrum, but had a burning need to learn why the salad dressing dilemma had even become a thing.

*Why couldn't I have the Italian dressing, and if "all food fits" then why was I forced to choose one food over the other? Ranch dressing is not fuel for the body; it makes no sense to sub it for the nutritional drink because they're non-comparable. It's like comparing apples to oranges; don't you get that? And if you already know that I prefer non-dairy items to those items containing dairy due to skin trouble, why would you force me to select the damn dressing that contains dairy?*

I was glad Scarlet was one of the therapists working for Monday night's group treatment. Her magical words of wisdom had sparked my biggest EDTC "Ah ha!" moment yet, and I needed her once again.

And so the saying goes, "ask and you shall receive."

Scarlet introduced an idea that once again really sat well with me, partially because I'd become quite trusting of Scarlet's insight and because I was able to wrap my head around something that seemed so false and felt so uncomfortable. She enabled my enraging experience to become a lesson learned.

Eating according to an "all food fits" philosophy is about taking all judgment away from food, regardless if you love the food, hate it or just deem it tolerable.

The work brings you to an uncomfortable place due to challenges faced when learning to accept foods that seem unsafe. You have to branch out from old eating habits and F.E.A.R.–based thoughts about food. Once again, black-and-white thinkers have to shift away from judgment and into a mentality of gray eating and gray thoughts about meals.

For example, black-and-white thinkers may not want the apple on the plate and would rather eat dinner without the apple being near their food. But the apple is being served and so that's got to be OK, and black-and-white thinkers must be cool with eating the apple although it may not be the "perfect" component.

Just one night later, I finished a meal at home that triggered a desire for more food. I was full, but the food didn't fully satisfy my expectations. My meal was basically breakfast for dinner, which provides a balanced and generally "safe" plate of food.

Two scrambled organic, cage-free, omega-3-rich, humanely-raised, high-in-protein eggs that are a great source of vitamin D, E, B12, B2 and B5. A handful of organic berries. A cup of diced potatoes with a pinch of pink Himalayan sea salt and organic garlic for flavor. My incorporation of a gray food choice was the potatoes—they weren't organic and contained disodium pyrophosphate to maintain color and potassium sorbate and sodium bisulfite to maintain freshness. The thought of preservatives made me cringe with nausea and fear, but it was also an act of bravery. Obviously, I survived consumption of the shit-filled potatoes and lived to tell.

Even though the potatoes weren't anything to write home about, I felt the strongest urge to have another, different dose of potatoes—the Alexia brand, organic, non–GMO crinkle-cut fries that come perfectly dusted with sea salt and bake to a scrumptious crisp. Certified USDA organic, free of preservatives, free of artificial colors … if I could just get my fix from those clean, flavorful French fries, my night would be complete. And it would really top things off if I finished off the whole bag—all five servings it contains.

*Stop, Holly. This is your eating disorder talking. You've had enough to eat, and you have to be OK with the potatoes you ate even though they were just OK. You do not need to fix the meal or make it perfect. It's fine just the way it is—it was just OK and you've got to be cool with the less-than-perfect outcome.*

**I will look forward. I will look forward.**

When food and things other than eating bring perfectionists into an uncomfortable, negative place, they tend to protect themselves from the negative emotions, usually by a not-so-great strategy that they've grown to trust.

It's important for black-and-white thinkers to be able to change the channel, sometimes very quickly, and find something uplifting. Think drama to comedy, like *Law & Order: SVU* to *Will and Grace*.

# CHAPTER 11

# Day Eight
## *Wednesday, August 9*

What if I told you that you must follow a number of guidelines in order to live a healthy life?

Makes sense, right?

There are practices, choices and routines that are backed by science and research, like getting a suitable amount of exercise, nutrition and sleep, which we must live by to maintain some degree of health.

But what about other guidelines that society has come to believe, which are actually not proven to maintain a healthy lifestyle, via marketing messages, trending topics on social media, irresponsible news reports and snippets about health heard from peers?

Well, folks, they're called dieting myths. I repeat, MYTHS. The EDTC's viewpoints are so very different from the myths heard so often by so many people. Those living with an eating disorder are more susceptible to latch onto certain myths and form an unbreakable bond.

Wednesday's treatment helped build the case against beliefs that I'd become married to, with loyalty that I'd never think about breaking. Some myths and I were meant to be together forever, to have and to hold, in sickness and in health.

According to EDTC philosophy, a strong commitment to dieting myths is a big part of where food judgment comes from. If we choose to believe an idea, we judge food based on what we believe it will do to our bodies.

An example: fat-free food is the healthiest choice.

In all reality, a calorie is a calorie is a calorie. Fat-free food is not a healthier version of fat-containing food. It shouldn't be chosen as the better-for-you alternative. When fat is removed, something has to be added to make up for the subtraction. So that means the low-fat or fat-free choice isn't the preferred option, according to professor Kerin O'Dea, director of the Samson Institute for Health Research at the University of South Australia.

O'Dea says low-fat foods are likely processed foods that you need to be careful with. Extra sugars are often added to make up for the loss of taste and texture that's caused when fat is removed.

Sugar and salt, as additives to improve taste and texture, are strongly linked to high blood pressure, which is super risky when it comes to having heart attacks and strokes.

Another myth people believe: more cardio = more weight loss.

Please take a break from the treadmill and pavement pounding. Even though decades of chatter told people that cardio was the fastest way to lose weight, that's actually not the case.

Research shows that after lifting weights for just one workout, your metabolism can be boosted for up to 36 hours. Let's say you burn 60 calories per hour while idle or inactive, so a weight training session would increase that burned calorie count to 70. Multiply that by 36 hours, and you'll see that the product is a big difference in your daily calorie expenditure.

Regular participation in weight lifting sessions will increase calorie burning and thus your body's fat burning capacity.

With cardio, you get an extra 40–80 calories burned after a moderate-paced session, but in order to generate a high amount of post-workout calorie burn, you'd have to be in motion for a really long, unrealistic period of time.

Generally, cardio training can help you slowly lose weight, but that weight loss will be a combination of fat AND muscle. When you perform resistance training and weight training, you have a better chance of losing only body fat.

Gluten-free foods are behind some mythical dieting beliefs, disguising themselves as a better option than foods containing gluten.

In recent years, local grocery store chains have placed gluten-free foods in the same section as all-natural, organic, "healthier" selections. They're also in the section where people with special diet needs can find food they're able to eat, like dairy-free alternatives and vegetarian-friendly entrees. Truth be told, gluten-free does NOT equal guilt-free. A gluten-free item is not at all healthier than a food containing gluten.

Some people are, in fact, allergic to gluten. They have a health condition that makes gluten consumption have very bad impacts on their bodies and on their health. For example, individuals with celiac disease must avoid gluten. The Celiac Disease Foundation defines the illness as a serious autoimmune disease that can occur in genetically predisposed people where the ingestion of gluten leads to damage of the small intestine. If and when the small intestine is attacked (which happens from an immune response to gluten), nutrients cannot be absorbed into the body, and it can cause unbearable abdominal pain.

Unless you have a gluten allergy, give yourself a green light for eating foods that are made with gluten.

Let's cover one more myth: carbs are the ultimate evil in weight gain.

Carbohydrates are NOT bad. And your body needs them. The Mayo Clinic recognizes that carbs have a bad rep when it comes to weight management, but carbs belong in your diet.

Carbs are your body's chief source of energy. As they're digested, they're turned into simple sugars and then absorbed into your blood stream as glucose. Your body turns to helpful glucose to power through activity, whether it's exercise or mental focus.

Fiber found in carbs may protect your body against obesity and type 2 diabetes.

Carbs consumed when you eat fruits, vegetables and whole grains don't lead to weight gain; instead, they help you control your weight. The Mayo Clinic says there are too few studies to believe that a diet rich in carbs will cause weight gain.

An additional fact check during Wednesday's session particularly hit home for me: the myth (YES, I SAID MYTH) that all-natural, clean, organic foods make you feel better and function better than foods that are not.

EDTC dieticians say that as an example, think of a processed food like bread. When people eat a piece of processed bread, they still get essential vitamins, proteins and carbs. The EDTC says that instead of worrying about every ingredient and being fearful of how processed foods might impact our bodies, it's far more important to make sure we have nutrition. All foods—no matter how natural or processed they are—provide some form of nutrition and nourishment.

By living according to the fearless, non-attachment of the "all food fits" lifestyle, you can live with the freedom of acceptance. Just think of the possibilities!

Oftentimes, someone with an eating disorder faces a lot of difficulty when trying to eat in various situations and settings. Let's say you're committed to eating only organic foods. What do you do when you're at a party, on a first date, or at a charity event (or YOUR favorite occasion)? Most public gatherings and restaurants do not and will not cater to an all-organic diet. Maybe it's the philosophy, increased food costs, or popular demand of customers but the majority of restaurants serve processed food.

The "all food fits" mentality makes everything ... well, just a whole lot easier. When you open your mind to accept nutrition from all foods, you allow yourself to be free—free to enjoy food and be present in the moment with the food. It might not be the food you prefer, but it's serving your body with the good "stuff" needed to live fully.

Someone with an eating disorder has very rigid thinking about food. For someone with an eating disorder who's also a black-and-white thinker, it's worse. Black-and-white thinkers put labels on every food item they encounter: good food or bad food. And when life takes a black-and-white thinker into a situation where bad food is offered, he or she experiences serious urges to restrict. The EDTC gradually pulls patients away from those urges and pushes them into places where eventually they accept all food. There's no longer good or bad food. There's just food—simple as that.

EDTC dieticians plan meals according to macronutrient consumption: a strategically laid-out combination of protein, carbs and fats.

And all those dieting myths ... they change how someone with an eating disorder sees a macronutrient-based diet. With so many fads and phases that come and go, the dieting industry puts the majority of its money into marketing and promotion of whatever fad is the hottest at that time. Society is flooded with info that ALL seems believable. We're so damn gullible as a society.

"Yes, I do feel so much better after removing 'x' from my diet!"

Well, then their friends try it ... and then friends of those friends

**From August 2016: A look inside my fridge, filled with only foods I deemed healthy, clean and "safe."**

try it … and it snowballs to all the friends of the friends. This is how a condition known as orthorexia nervosa—an unhealthy obsession with healthy eating, or a fixation on righteous eating—can begin. Someone impacted by orthorexia starts out by attempting to eat healthier, but then becomes hooked on, and obsessed with, food quality and purity.

The National Eating Disorders Association says orthorexia causes people to be overly preoccupied with what and how much they eat and how to deal with "slip-ups."

*"An iron-clad will is needed to maintain this rigid eating style. Every day is a chance to eat right, be 'good,' rise above others in dietary prowess, and self-punish if temptation wins (usually through stricter eating, fasts and exercise). Self-esteem becomes wrapped up in the purity of orthorexics' diet and they sometimes feel superior to others, especially in regard to food intake.*

*Eventually food choices become so restrictive, in both variety and calories, that health suffers—an ironic twist for a person so completely dedicated to healthy eating. Eventually, the obsession with healthy eating can crowd out other activities and interests, impair relationships, and become physically dangerous."*

The work done through EDTC's Partial Hospitalization and Intensive Outpatient treatment changes the way patients think about food. It breaks obsessions, dissolves guilt and releases fear that holds patients back from enjoying all foods. The brains of patients can be adjusted and changed, but the way to achieve transformation is by doing the opposite of what feels comfortable.

*I have to change what I buy at the grocery store.*
*I have to change the times of day I eat.*
*I have to change what I define as a healthy meal.*
*I have to change my intentions and goals of eating.*
*I have to change my feelings about what food does to my body and mind.*
*I have to stop judging food.*

I realized on that Wednesday night that I had to create a new path to utilize, continue to use and maintain new thoughts about food so that my "all food fits" way of life would keep functioning.

It takes just the right materials to build a new road. New neuropathways in and out of the brain mean following a new plan—one that challenges beliefs and keeps my eating disorder from taking hold and taking control. ***I will look forward. I will look forward.***

# CHAPTER 12

# Day Nine

### *Saturday, August 12*

I had every reason to open my eyes and explode out of bed Saturday morning, erupting with excitement to spend that afternoon and Sunday with my best friend Pamela and her two youngest kids. Let me preface, I'm not a kid person, but I adore nine-year-old Nate and six-year-old Aubrey. We were all set for a fun-filled couple of days, and just being able to see my BFF of 15 years was every reason to be happy.

But I wasn't cheerful. I was in a nasty funk. Not that I wasn't looking forward to seeing Pamela; I was just far from feeling like a morning at the EDTC.

Isn't it something when you're in a bad mood, and a few things happen to spark your anger and make things worse (rhetorical question)? It was like I was preset to expect to get ticked off.

First, I showed up at 8:58 a.m. to an empty waiting room, soon to be joined by Elise, who hadn't said a word in more than a week. Yet, when she was allowed under EDTC guidelines, she listened to music blaring through her ear buds and the only things able to make eye contact with Elise were the floor and her lap. Her recent bad mood and negative vibe had sent me straight into a rut, and on that Saturday morning, the rut was very hard to handle. I wanted Elise to be happy. I didn't want her to be hurt or depressed by whatever may have been going on in her life, but helping Elise seemed way out of the question. I was afraid to try, afraid she would reject my support.

Once I stepped foot inside the treatment room, I observed that the air was considerably stuffy, and I was incredibly thankful for the clear, plain, acceptable water bottle that wouldn't be denied by EDTC staff.

Think about this for a minute: have you ever imagined that filling up a 16.9-ounce water bottle from a water dispenser could be considered a crime? At the EDTC, I guess it can. I was escorted to the cafeteria and with eagle eyes over my every move, I was granted permission to fill up my within-standards water bottle.

You guessed it—mood tumbles further downhill and hits a few tree branches along the way.

My therapist (a.k.a. water warden) also decided that moment was the prime time to send another dose of shit my way: my laptop computer that I brought to treatments and used to take notes ... well, that would be no more. No computers, no phones. If I wanted to take notes, it would have to happen via putting pen to paper.

*Now I'm absolutely pissed off. Did I mention that I can't write as quickly as I can type? So now what—you want to subtract something else from what I'm able to do here? This is my book we're talking about. Its content ... and quality of information ... depend on my notes taken during treatment.... I must use notes to record each session and big takeaways from exercises and discussions. If the value and worth of my content suffers, this book will suffer, and HOW DARE YOU stand in the way of my dream?*

I wanted to bolt out of the EDTC. I wanted my morning to have been filled with happiness, not the bullshit thrown at me by EDTC beliefs and policies. My anger told me to launch the water bottle hard enough against a wall so that it exploded and sent water flying everywhere. It told me to kick the nearby wall with so much force that a hole would be left behind.

My face felt like it had been instantly scorched. The tingling of anger raced up and down my forearms. I picked at any part of my fingernails I could get ahold of. I ground my lower teeth against the back of my top middle teeth, as if the all these nervous habits would alleviate the anxiety and anger that were taking me through a torture chamber.

GET ME OUT OF HERE.

*Wait, Holly, stop. Your therapist is just doing her job. There's a reason—even if it's unknown to you at this time—behind monitoring the water station and forbidding the use of electronics.*

*Remember:* **I will look forward. I will look forward.**

A loud sigh, gladly, was enough for a quick fix of my anger, and with a heavy march I returned to the treatment room for Saturday morning's exercise.

According to EDTC therapists, a big portion of their patients say they don't even know who they are outside of their eating disorder, and that because of the mental illness, they've lost themselves. When values become those caused by an eating disorder, they can actually take over what people find essential and necessary for health and happiness.

For Saturday's exercise, I compared my core values to my eating disorder values—important work to get my priorities in check and distinguish them from what my eating disorder tells me is important.

**My Values:** Optimal health, optimal nutrition, cleanliness, happiness, high energy level, balance, peace, love.

*I want to eat as healthy as possible, acquiring as much nutrition as I can. I want to feel clean on the inside, unhampered by an upset stomach, foggy mind or weakened spirit. I want to experience pure happiness every day.*

*I want vibrant, elevated energy to keep me highly productive and motivated to consistently perform at my best. I want balance—work hard, play hard, rest hard. I want to feel like others love me for who I am.* **I want to live a radiant and peaceful life—a life free of worry and full of love.**

**Eating Disorder Values:** Competition, over-achievement, perfection, indulgence, inadequacy.

*I want to be the best and I need to eat foods that will help me be the best.*

*I need to eat a perfect slate of clean foods, allowing for no fried foods, dairy, processed foods, non-organic ingredients, chemicals, additives or excessive sugar, and so I'll restrict where needed to maintain this diet.*

*I can't let anything take away from perfect standards or habits: to-do lists must be completed, beauty must be constantly worked for, I can't forget anything or make any mistakes and so I'll have to make sure nothing falls by the wayside and that I never fall short of my expectations. If I make a mistake or let myself down, I might as well make the most of it and call the entire day a wash, and so I'll get in all my cravings within one day so that I can start the new day on a fresh, clean, once-again-perfect slate, and leave the scars of imperfection in the past.*

When you live with an eating disorder, it's a constant battle between each set of values: you at your core vs. you with your eating disorder. You try desperately to fight for your values, protecting them from your eating disorder's attacks and attempts to destroy everything you once knew to be true, and just because of its irrefutable strength, the eating disorder pulls you away from your values that allow you to feel good. As the distance expands and your values get farther and farther away, so does your ability to feel good (whatever good means to you—that depends on your individual values).

Because of my eating disorder and its tendency to invite itself to the party whenever it chooses to, values of health and nutrition, cleanliness, happiness, energy, balance and peace are oftentimes way out of my reach. **No matter how high I jump or how far I leap, I just can't touch what's really important to me—things that make my soul sing, things that motivate me and things that help me look forward to tomorrow.**

The struggle, from time to time, brings me to complete isolation … and although I'm a part-time introvert, more often than not, I am an extrovert—loud and proud! Isolation was opposite of my real self's truth: I want to be in a crowd, at an event…. I want to have a total blast…. I love letting my social butterfly soar and letting the energy of others motivate me.

Instead of living authentically, I find every dishonest excuse in the book to keep me "safe" from harm. I can't go because I have a deadline. I can't go because I have to do "x" or "y." I can't go because I might be going out of town. I can't go because I have some catching up to do. I can't go because I need to write my book … or…. I just don't return calls or texts because I don't want to tell a lie.

But truth be told, it hurts too much to be vulnerable, to inch out of my comfort zone, to risk being put to shame, and to feel the social anxiety that makes me feel like a disgrace.

*To any friend I've ever hurt by not showing up: I am so incredibly, deeply sorry.*

Believe it or not, I spent nearly two years as a health and fitness writer and editor for a major news outlet in Cincinnati. I produced reliable, educational information about the latest and greatest in health and fitness. In that role, my face and name were attached to numerous news stories. And because of the pride that came with my job, and the responsibility I had in providing life-changing information, I maintained identification as a source of how to eat well and live your best life through diets and fitness. In fact, the company branded my stories "Healthy Living."

The job fueled my competitive spirit. I felt that if I'm eating better and living better than others, then that meant I was a better person. And if I put the real me out there, it would have negated the person I'd come to be: the Healthy Living expert. It was a F.E.A.R.–based thought that I had to lead by example and live a certain way when in the eyes of my newsroom colleagues. And let me tell you … pizza and cake are VERY frequent visitors to newsrooms. And man, I wanted the pizza and cake. My mouth watered. But during my time as Healthy Living expert at that news station, I never dared take one bite.

It's like the saying "If I could have known then what I know now." It would have been totally cool to be a fitness guru who ALSO likes pizza and cake, but my fears had blinded me to the possibility, no matter how simple it seems now.

Moral of the story: eating disorder behaviors are NOT aligned with who we really are. Think of an extroverted person working in a lonely library, having her energy sucked dry by solitude. It's just not a match. But when you have an eating disorder, you go on about your day, and before you know it, your eating disorder becomes your identity because for such a long time, **your time and energy went toward your eating disorder identity … not your real self.**

Just as Saturday had started out, snack time also failed to go down without a fight. The food selection for snack was lined up as usual, with my oh-so-safe banana right up front waiting for me. I'd watched a Cheez-Its commercial earlier that week, reminding me how good the classic snack cracker tasted, so I grabbed a snack-size bag of Cheez-Its to finish my mid-morning snack.

Still on the grumpy side, I sat down with the other folks of Saturday morning's group and of course, soon came the supervisors, making sure we got the appropriate goods.

Of all days, of all times … sure enough, my selection was wrong. The crackers, as I was told, counted as two Exchanges and I was only allowed one Exchange based on my dietician's meal plan for me.

I didn't want to go back and choose again. Choosing dialed up my anxiety and it was there in no time—just like a first responder's arrival to an accident.

"You know what, how about you just get me something that counts as one Exchange," I said. "Get me something that will be right and I'll just eat that."

Of course, no supervisor was going to select my snack for me, so there I went, the same sigh released once again in frustration and disgust, along with a few choice words under my breath.

So get this ... once everyone finishes snack, EDTC supervisors make sure you've eaten all of it. They literally pressed down on my snack bag and squished my banana peel to make sure that I had completed every last bite of my food.

I wasn't sure how much more I could take. The EDTC's supervision seemed ridiculous and made me feel like a complete fool.

The last half of Saturday included a TED Talk video, but my poor attitude and short temper kept me from watching the speech. My eyes were there, but my focus was on my anger, confusion and resentment. I'm not even sure who the speaker was ... needless to say, I wasn't paying attention.

Per the group discussion once the TED Talk ended, its main topic was about being vulnerable, which, astoundingly, #nailedit with my dating life at that time, and really any kind of relationship I tried to have.

I've lived with an "I'm not good enough" roof over my head since I was about 12 or 13 years old and in the 7th grade. My best friend Lucy, from my first year in middle school, decided she didn't want to be my best friend anymore. Instead, she wanted to be Ashley's best friend.

I felt the biggest absence without Lucy to talk to between classes, to share our secret handshake every day after school, and to have slumber parties on the weekends. We were inseparable, and with Lucy gone, I spent the 7th grade trying to separate myself from crushed feelings.

Not only had my best friend (BFFAEAEAA—best friend forever and ever and ever and always) decided I was total shit with nothing to offer and no qualities that were worthy of friendship, but she and her new crew were so mean to me. They bullied me in the cafeteria at lunch, left nasty notes in my locker, and spread dreadful rumors about me. Before I knew it, going to school had turned into an "I'm not good enough" nightmare.

I never asked Lucy why she'd distanced herself from me—I never found the bravery to confront her. I was also afraid of what she might say.

Insecurity became my new best friend … and it never left my side. More than 20 years later, we're still attached at the hip.

Something so tough, even as a kid, can have an appalling impact on a person's development. The experience sticks with you, and even as an adult, its lasting impact seems impossible to escape from.

So there you have it. My F.E.A.R.–based belief—I'm not good enough—not for family, colleagues, teammates, friends, romantic partners, you name it. Sometimes, I'm not even good enough for me.

So you can imagine how terrifying it is to be vulnerable—to risk actually experiencing the feeling that "I'm not good enough." If being vulnerable means allowing yourself to be seen in an "as is" state, there's absolutely NO WAY I'm willing and/or able. So for decades I've strived for perfection and haven't settled, not once. I try to settle for what seems "just OK," but that achievement renders itself impossible. It's like I could have scored an A in the class, but I'm trying to accept a C+ instead. Until I feel like I have no room for improvement, my relationships and potential to gain relationships is severely hindered. At this time, I'm emotionally unable to handle rejection. It's happened too much, too often without explanation. It's the reason why I isolate and why being by myself feels more lonely than I can bear.

Rejection and the fear that follows have pushed me into an unbreakable pattern and lifestyle of black-and-white thinking. I want people to like me, accept me and love me, but fear tells me that I must present a perfect person with a perfect life for that to happen, because if I'm flawless, only then will I be good enough for others.

## CHAPTER 13

# Day 10

## *Monday, August 14*

I didn't go. I couldn't go.

I needed, in the worst way, to press the pause button and take an evening for myself, and so Monday marked my first missed treatment session.

I played hooky. Guilty as charged.

I felt bad about deciding to skip. I had a heavy conscience riding on my shoulders, reminding me all day long, over and over, that I wasn't doing the right thing—that I wasn't stepping up to the plate, and that I was taking the easy way out.

But my body and mind spoke very loudly, telling me that I was lethargic, run down, overwhelmed. It was like I needed a recharge more than I needed air.

Have you ever spent a wonderful weekend away that was powerfully enjoyable and insightful, and you brought the impact of that experience back to your "real" life?

That's pretty much what went down during the two weekend days before that missed EDTC evening. I'd spent the weekend in Louisville, Kentucky, with Pamela. She's married with two kids of her own, and two from her husband Joe's previous marriage.

As of summer 2017, the friendship between Pamela and me was 15 years strong. We have the type of friendship that's hard to find—the kind in which you can go for a few months without talking, and when you finally connect, you pick right back up as if no time was lost. We've been through undergrad at the University of Kentucky; enjoyed fun college times (we'll save those details for another day); suffered broken hearts; survived a highway car accident that sent us underneath a semi-truck and out the other side (we walked away with exceptionally minor injuries); been through both our parents' divorces; and endured family members' funerals. I've gladly been a part of her family and her children's lives. Of course, we've also shared countless tears, uncontrollable laughs and memories made while dancing the night away.

I've always admired, and I admit, envied how Pamela always seems to have it together, have it all figured out. She's more go with the flow and laid-back than I could ever dream of being. I've had to remind myself on numerous occasions that I can't let jealousy creep into our priceless friendship … even though it truly seems like Pamela has it all: the most ideal, abundant life filled with so much fortune and love. Instead of wishing aspects of my life were different so that I can experience some of Pamela's joy, I've learned to use Pamela's disposition, knowledge and attitude to help my outlook be a little brighter when it becomes dim.

**Pamela (right) and me at a Corbin, Kentucky, auto repair shop after the undeniably scary underneath-semi-truck-accident in March 2016.**

This past weekend was a prime example of Pamela's wonderful influence. We talked a lot about black-and-white thinking, and the gray area I'm taking baby steps into. We talked about competitive natures and how the need to be the best adds unthinkable pressure to our lives. I invited her relaxed, even-keeled vibes to defeat a lot of my anxiety … and I wasn't ready, just one day later, to let the EDTC steal my joy.

Call it a sign of rebellion should you choose, but the program kept a constant gloomy cloud over me as a reminder that I was messed up and needed mental health help, and I wanted nothing to do with that *gray* cloud on Monday.

I couldn't … I wouldn't … report back to that Cincinnati building with its half-musty office/half-hospital smell to announce my mood, irritability and anxiety to a group of people who weren't my close friends. I wouldn't willingly participate in an exercise meant to strengthen my self-esteem and body image. I wouldn't choke down a meal that was selected for me without my preference meaning a damn thing. And I wouldn't sit around in a group circle trying desperately to remain calm while reacting to my experience at dinner and "sharing my feelings."

Not tonight, EDTC. Not tonight.

Instead, I wanted the freedom to spend my Monday evening as I chose, not how the EDTC chose. I wanted to enjoy a meal (sans binge episode) without hawks watching me put food on a plate and eat it. I wanted my breathing to be slow and natural, instead of the anxiety-filled, on-edge breaths I tend to take at the EDTC. I wanted a fun evening at the gym with a friend, rather than an evening at the EDTC where, even among peers, I feel utterly alone.

The one-night break was ideal because it gave me just that: a break. When I left the office right at 5 p.m., I chose to hit the gym, prepare and enjoy my own meal, and then just relax. Sit there. Get lost in the evening's entertainment news reports on TV. Wear foul-patterned pajama pants and an old t-shirt that didn't match. Pile zit cream on the "friend" that found its way onto the apple of my right (face) cheek. Watch the sun set from my balcony. Actually do the unheard of thing that is unwinding before falling into to bed.

Admittedly, I didn't feel *perfectly* centered after my one-night hiatus from the EDTC. It was a nice break, but the thought of facing possible punishment for "skipping school" haunted me. Plus, I knew treatment wasn't over and I'd have to get back on track in order to fully recover. I also knew that treatment had begun empowering me to let go of impossible expectations, experience a bit of forgotten freedom regarding food and be nicer to myself.

*I will look forward.*

The break from treatment was temporary, but it made permanent progress in my journey away from perfection.

How about this for a conclusion to Monday: **I no longer have perfect attendance … wait for it…. I'm in the gray area of attendance. And I'm OK with that.**

# CHAPTER 14

# Day 11

## *Wednesday, August 16*

I grew up in a Southern Baptist home, and because my parents were strict and sheltered me like you wouldn't believe, I was raised according to very strong morals. We had plenty of traditions to carry out from year to year. Some of them I liked; some of them, not so much.

I learned at a young age that I better not dare tell a lie. So I don't lie. Period. I've never been able to fib, and even when I've tried, I'm so terrible at telling a lie that I get busted right from the get-go. I might be brutally truthful at times, but dishonesty is a bone that I do not have in my body.

So when I showed up to the EDTC on Wednesday, I was prepared to tell the truth about my Monday absence. I saw my therapist before group treatment, and when she asked if I felt better, I confidently let her

I didn't want to smile for the camera, or wear that outfit, as a five-year-old having my portrait made in August 1987.

know that I wasn't ill, but that I needed the night away. A bit to my surprise, there was no backlash or judgment, and Carmen didn't seem at all doubtful or perturbed. I breathed a sigh of relief to start the evening, but I still had reservations built up inside.

As I've had little faith in psychologists before, I was ready to see more out of my meetings with Carmen. I wanted to see her professional skills put to work and I needed to get clear on results and how therapy would get me there. I linked the idea of instant gratification to therapy and felt impatient … almost unwilling to go through months of treatment because—let's face it—Carmen doesn't know me. Can't family, mentors and friends give me fitting advice because they're the ones who know Holly Pennebaker inside and out?

It was like Carmen had read my mind. We opened right into the real conversation that desperately needed to happen. We talked about Saturday's angering episodes—the supervised water bottle fill-up and the denial of use of my laptop for notes.

*Don't treat me like I'm incapable of being trusted, that I'm unable to make general decisions! If I want to walk to the water machine and fill up my label-free water bottle, then let me do it in peace! Yes—there's food in the kitchen (where the water machine is located), and I get that some patients will attempt to steal food, hide food, quickly consume that food … but that's not me! If others need to be watched, then watch them. But I don't need that kind of supervision! I don't need to be stared at during my every move of filling up a water bottle!*

What was interesting wasn't the discussion of my reaction to the overbearing supervision, but it was the next layer that made me swallow a gulp of pride so big I could have choked.

Why couldn't I have asked—right there in the moment—about the supervised water fetch?

I could have said, *"You know, it makes me feel like you don't trust me when I get water to drink. It makes me feel like I'm unable to do the right thing. Can we talk about this?"*

That doesn't sound so bad, right?

The transformation had just set in—right there, right then.

I'm absolutely awful at real conversations in the moment, even though some folks, like my editor Mike, might argue against that claim.

Even well before the tough conversation takes place, I create possible

F.E.A.R.–based directions the conversation could take and what my reaction would need to be in order to maintain the state of being correct or to convince the other person(s) to see my point. And if the real conversation were to get heated and morph into a dispute, I'd already have my opposing arguments ready to fire off. No matter what the conversation's counterpart might have ready, my weapon would protect me from vulnerability, the chance of being defeated and the chance of being hurt.

If the fierce conversation catches me off guard, I don't stop and think to ask questions or to meet the other person halfway. I get mad, my anger goes from zero to 60 in a split second, I say something that I'll eventually regret, and I run away. I avoid the uncomfortable situation, and I instantly make it an "end of the world" scenario.

And I know exactly why: the uncomfortable situation—the conflict—is in a gray area. My mindset looks at those times like either all things are good and agreed on or all things are bad and there's complete disagreement. Agreeing to disagree? Likely not happening.

I don't have a need to be right, for I know it's far better to be happy. And one thing Carmen was entirely right about on Wednesday was that I had to find a way to control that anger and be OK when things got gray. Sure, we're not all always going to get along ... but that meeting with Carmen told me, in the most humbling way, that I don't quite have the backbone and tolerance for pressure that I thought I had.

Wednesday's Process session, during which the floor opened up for patients to seek support from peers in addition to discuss meals, built on my talk with Carmen and it definitely wasn't planned that way. One of those "meant to be" moments!

A newcomer to the group, Ruth, was having trouble getting proper support from her small group of coworkers to help her overcome her eating disorder. Because they had a close working relationship and friendship too, from the way Ruth described it, she chose to let them know about her decision to seek treatment. Ruth said when it came time for lunch, her coworkers took on an unwelcomed "mom" role and overdid the effort to help make sure Ruth ate properly.

"Did you eat a carb?" Ruth said they asked her.

She said she felt constant eyes on her at lunchtime, watching to make sure she didn't skip the meal. But it was too much to handle, and Ruth was bogged down in stress about what to do.

To help Ruth, we discussed a "DEAR MAN" technique to handle conflict, especially during times of eating disorder struggle. When someone has an eating disorder, their ability to handle conflict is impacted—they can be highly sensitive and more reserved than usual, and they can have a tendency to get defensive. When you have an eating disorder, you're very aware that something is wrong … that you're sick … but you're also working so hard to hide it and fix it on your own that emotions and conflict don't mix—at all.

DEAR MAN is an acronym:

D—Describe the situation.

E—Express yourself, make it clear what you need.

A—Assert, remembering that others can't read your mind.

R—Reinforce or reward by explaining positive impacts of getting what you need.

M—Mindful. Keep your focus on your goals, maintain your position.

A—Appear confident and competent, and use strong eye contact.

N—Negotiate by being willing to give. Focus on what will work. Ask: What do you think we should do?

Asking someone for what you need can be difficult, regardless of whether you have a mental illness. What might the grim conversation do to the relationship if, in fact, the tough talk has enough power to change the relationship's vibe?

In addition to DEAR MAN, the EDTC therapists recommend a specific format to begin the conversation:

"When you _____, I feel _____, because _____, and I need _____."

I'll use my pet peeve as an example: tardiness!

*"When you're late, I feel like you don't care about your time with me, because your time was spent elsewhere, and I need to know that you care about being with me."*

I took some time later that week to reflect on my failure to handle conflict well, and what role that could have played in my failed relationships. **On a larger scale, how could the pain of mental illness drive precious relationships to failure?**

*Friends:*

*I'm so sorry that I didn't just take a simple step back and talk to you calmly. I'm sorry that I got offended so easily and came up with my own conclusion that I wasn't important to you and that you didn't care about me. I'm sorry I went for months without talking to you because it was easier to go with my assumption and push you away than to reach out and have a tough talk. I'm sorry if you felt like I no longer cared. I've cared more than you could ever know. I've sobbed over the loss of you from my life and I've felt the stabbing pains of loneliness, for much of which I'm responsible.*

*I'm sorry that I felt like our friendship had entered a gray area and that I tunneled away instead of facing my fear of conflict. I'm sorry we don't talk anymore, that I don't know what you're up to right now, and that we've been absent from each other's lives. I'm going through quite a bit of transformation right now and I'm getting help for a mental illness that's destroying the person who I hope to be one day. Right now, I'm spending some time alone because I cry often and I don't want you to see that.*

*Right now, I'm trying to accept myself for having an eating disorder and it's difficult beyond belief. Right now, I'm living day to day, trying to manage suffocating anxiety. Right now, I'm afraid I can't be fun enough to hang out with because I'm working through the excruciating weight on my heart. Right now, I'm afraid to be vulnerable and I'm afraid I won't be good enough for you. Know that you are so very special and important to me, and that you'll always have a place in my life and in my heart.*

# CHAPTER 15

# Day 12

## *Saturday, August 19*

Our bodies are not made to get stuck in a rut. They're made to move.

Our minds are not made to be still. They're made to experience practices and understandings and also to grow.

Those pieces of empowerment from Saturday morning's Rise and Flow yoga class were all I needed to hear, first to validate the 6:15 a.m. wake-up alarm and second to prepare my mind and set an intention for the upcoming morning treatment at the EDTC.

I felt strong and confident, proud and content. I was ready to be open, flexible and optimistic.

Part of that sky-high feeling was due to a fun first date on Thursday night and an awesome AcroYoga workshop on Friday night—both of which forced me out of my comfort zone and into the world of taking chances, playing with the unknown.

Needless to say, both occasions were outstanding successes!

Back to the lecture at hand…

A peculiar, discouraging "buzz kill" set in during the hour between yoga and my EDTC arrival. The familiar feeling of not wanting to go was there, of course, but this time it was more intense—strong enough to cause anger and initiate a terrible attitude. The EDTC was bringing me down from a few days of considerable confidence. I didn't want to succumb to feeling judged and misunderstood, which had started to become a pattern. I didn't want to accept limitations like the forbidden use of my laptop, the frowning upon my phone being out of my handbag, and the unheard-of restroom trip taking place within 30 minutes of the last time I ate.

**Yoga friends Tonya (bottom), Heather and I partnered for a triple plank at the AcroYoga workshop in August 2017.**

Yes, patients must wait 30 minutes before using the restroom after a meal or snack. It took me several treatment sessions before I realized why that rule was in place. Turns out, if patients practice purging behaviors, they're most likely to purge soon after eating. The longer food is in your system, the more difficult it is to purge. I admit, it's frustrating when I need to legitimately use the restroom but can't because of the EDTC policy. I'm not one to purge so why do I have to be treated like someone who does?

*I will look forward. I will look forward.*

That Saturday, it was exceptionally difficult to accept the fact that I had to repeatedly show up for mental healthcare. It made me feel powerless, limited and different. For one, I felt like I was out of the eating disorder wheelhouse because I'd had little to no desire to binge over the last couple weeks. I felt like I was in control of my body and that my urges to binge had stepped away … at least for the time being.

"Why would you take ibuprofen if you don't have a headache?" I asked during Saturday's check-in.

I told the group that I felt like I didn't have an eating disorder; it was like it had gone away. I was eating healthy, nutritious and smart. I was seeing the change in my body as the binge eating had stopped and I was on a good track with regular food consumption.

I also acknowledged the lack of truth behind those feelings, that they were more of a mask over the reality. Because an eating disorder is a long-term, often-permanent illness, I was sure it could and would walk right back into my life at some point down the road. That's what it does. From age 19 to 34, it ebbed and flowed. I knew that loneliness, depression, lack of work-life balance and absence of motivation triggered it. But I never, ever knew when the eating disorder would return.

That particular Saturday marked a morning where I had to search super hard for empathy toward the others in my treatment group. Mental illness is incredibly dangerous, and just because I'd felt better for two weeks didn't mean … well … it didn't mean a damn thing! Maybe my peers didn't feel better. I needed to be there for them, ready to provide support at any given moment. After all, the hard stuff is better battled when we fight TOGETHER.

I shared with the group that I would work to keep my mind in a place of acceptance of my eating disorder, where I know that I need help that will bring about change to last well into the future. Because I am mentally ill, I acknowledged that there's no quick fix and that although life was pretty good, I wasn't anywhere near out of the woods.

What I didn't know Saturday was that the group discussion would cover EXACTLY what the doctor ordered: answers to my questions about the long term and future healing, and the fact there's no "fix." **A disease doesn't come with repair instructions. Mental illness comes with tools to feel better throughout an ongoing process.**

I'd been so wrong. And so arrogant.

*Just sit there and take it, Holly. You're not better than anyone else.*

*You don't force yourself to vomit after you eat, but that doesn't mean you're better than your peer who does. The EDTC isn't going to fix you. It seems unfair that you have an eating disorder, but open up to the help that's right in front of your face. Get your nose out of the air. Knock the chip off your shoulder. Be thankful for the resources you have found within the EDTC. Just let go. Accept. Surrender.*

The group discussion was about relapse prevention. I don't even know what a binge-eating relapse would look like at this point, but I was sure as hell about to learn.

Lo and behold, Scarlet, the therapist who said things in a way that purely resonated and was the brains behind the spider analogy, walked in to lead the discussion. Something clicked and a switch turned on my optimism so easily in a split second. I knew what Scarlet had to teach would sit very well with me and that I would learn the lesson in a way that was effective. She just had an exceptional, special way of reaching me.

There are three stages of relapse prevention: slip, lapse and relapse.

Pavel G. Somov, Ph.D., uses a banana peel analogy to describe each stage in his adapted essay "The Bananas of Slip, Lapse and Re-Lapse Prevention," taken from *Recovery Equation* (Somov, Somova 2003–4). Somov applies it to any compulsive/addictive behavior.

The Slip is awareness. You're walking down a sidewalk and you see a banana peel. You realize that if you step on it, then you will slip and fall. The awareness of the potential fall is enough for you to choose to avoid the peel, and so you walk around it and continue your stroll. There's some internal debate happening in your mind: Do I do what's right and walk around the peel, or do I slip on the peel by engaging in an old eating disorder behavior?

"A slip is a moment of having a craving/desire to use but not using," according to Somov. "You want something but you can't have it or you are not allowing yourself to have it."

The Lapse is surrender. You're walking down a sidewalk and you don't see the slippery banana peel because you're not paying attention. You step on the peel, slip and lose your balance, but keep yourself from hitting the ground. You surrender to your food craving when you lapse, but you don't go so far as the condition that brought you to treatment. You momentarily slipped, but you were able to find strength and can get back up.

Somov writes, "A lapse means surrendering to the craving to use … having one substance [or food]-abusing episode."

The Relapse is repeated falling. You're walking down the sidewalk and like the lapse, you don't see the slippery banana peel, you step on it and lose your balance. However, this time, you can't regain control and you fall down. You put your hands and feet down, and then attempt to lift your body back up, but you might even fall again. Because the fall hurt pretty badly, you can't recapture balance, and you're too unsteady to get back on your feet. Taking the tumble causes you to grow weaker instead of dusting yourself off and getting back up again.

"Relapse is falling down and staying down … until you give up on trying," Somov says.

What came next was a black-and-white thinking lesson at its absolute finest.

According to Somov's work, "A catastrophized, all-or-nothing view [on a slip, lapse and relapse] is a truly disempowering and dehumanizing prognosis."

A relapse is not a regression back to square one, according to Somov. Instead, it's an entry into a gray area of mental illness. Someone with an eating disorder must not think in a black-and-white way when it comes to an eating disorder and the possibility of a slip, lapse or relapse. It's acceptable to give in and eat the food you've been craving, but then you move on, stronger than you were before, and as imperfect as you were before. Basically, in relapse prevention, it's not the end of the world if you slip up every now and then—that's how you build awareness, knowledge and strength so you can live with your eating disorder. Life goes on.

Sure, it's natural to look at the slip or the lapse and feel like you screwed up, but don't blow it out of proportion and do it again and again and again. Own your screw-up, accept it and move forward.

*I will look forward. I will look forward.*

It was a harsh reality to hear, but I had to face it: an eating disorder is a disease.

Medical treatment administered by a medical professional indicates that you're sick and a doctor cures you. Medicine is a quick fix for illness. Medicine is black and white. This belief in medicine, according to the EDTC, is an Americanized view of treating an illness. In other countries, treatment is provided more holistically and people learn to live with their disease and to live a healthy life, one in which the illness doesn't keep them down and out for the count.

Living free of black-and-white thinking, when you have a disease, is about learning to deal with the addiction and without feelings attached to the uncomfortable times spent in the gray areas. At times, you might want to go back to the addiction, but as long as you stick to your treatment plan for your eating disorder, and limit the times you slip, you will be OK in the long haul.

When you're in recovery, you can't be completely cured because that would represent black-and-white thinking.

In fact, there is no cure OR curable disease—this is black-and-white thinking, too. Every time you even think about your eating disorder, it means you're not cured. EDTC therapists understand there are plenty shades of gray. A slip does not equal a relapse. Give yourself a break. Recovery is an ongoing process.

It's OK to just be better. Don't expect to be healed, fixed or made perfect again—those pictures don't exist. They're F.E.A.R.–based thoughts, not your reality.

For example, my knowledge that loneliness, poor work-life balance and lack of motivation triggered my eating disorder should inform me that for an effective prevention plan, I need to be more engaged with people, avoid isolation and get out there when something fun is going down. The social activity will likely provoke an eating disorder because it makes me care about my looks. I want to look perfect when I attend a social event. I want my hair to be full and in place, my makeup to be a remarkable piece of art, and my clothes to represent a confident, comfortable, happy woman. My image, so I thought, should tell the world that I'm proud of who I am.

When a patient feels better, as I had been recently, chances are the eating disorder stuff is just hanging out—it's dormant. Still, there's a battle inside of you that has disappeared into the background. It's like the eating disorder has stopped its yelling, but still whispers. Above all, the eating disorder is present.

You cannot put pressure on yourself to think that eating disorder thoughts and behaviors will be gone someday because you've been in a battle. You have war wounds. You have scars. You've seen some scary stuff and now you carry a bit of baggage. Bandages and crutches are just part of life.

To ditch the black-and-white thinking, you have to understand residual things aren't necessarily gone. There's no such thing as "fixed." You have to learn how to effectively live with your body, in your body, and that includes all of your true self—even if some of that truth is difficult to accept. You must hear your eating disorder's commands in the voice it chooses to use, and you must be able to be louder than the eating disorder. You have to decide what you're going to do. You must be more powerful than the eating disorder.

*I am in control, eating disorder. You are not. You might still whisper and try to butt in, but you won't be loud enough and you're not welcome here. You won't be heard in a way that causes me to screw up my recovery process, and the goals I've worked so hard to accomplish along the way. I can ... and will ... say no to you.*

Once discussion ended, we headed to the cafeteria for snack time. I grabbed a green apple and a yogurt (yes, something that contains dairy ... and I was reluctant AND OK with that). I wanted the protein, knowing I'd exercised that morning and woken up ridiculously early for a Saturday.

There's something that happens at the end of the 15-minute snack break that gets under my skin more and more, week after week. An EDTC therapist literally checks to make sure we complete our snack ... like, eat every bite. She lifted the lid off my yogurt to prove I hadn't left any behind. She pushed down on Ruth's KIND Bar wrapper to make sure Ruth had eaten every crumb. And that check was the same for April's cottage cheese container, Elise's Goldfish snack pack, and so on. You can hear the crumbling of the foil packaging as it is smashed onto the table, making it crystal clear that no one left a morsel. The sounds of the food package inspections are like nails on a chalkboard and to see her hand in motion is like a slap in the face.

Saturday finished up by watching a TED Talk from Brene Brown which really hit home for much of my EDTC crew. The wheels were turning, and I could feel their rotation in my mind as realizations came to light and some things really started to make sense.

For starters, vulnerability does NOT equal weakness. Instead,

Brown says, vulnerability is an emotional risk. Vulnerability is exposure. Vulnerability is uncertainty.

Vulnerability is necessary to fuel our daily lives, as it's the most accurate measurement of courage.

By being vulnerable, we allow ourselves to be seen in an honest way—who we really are instead of who we *think* we're being in society. We might think society views us a certain way because that's how we're trying to carry ourselves—like we have it all figured out, we're perfectly put together, like we're unbreakable. In reality, we probably don't have it all figured out, we're far from perfect, and we've been broken and we're still broken.

No wonder I turned down my recent date in April. I wanted to show up looking flawless on the outside and I wanted a perfect life to present from the inside. And in April, that was way too scary to fathom. So another little tidbit from Thursday's first date: I showed up with a huge zit on the apple of my right cheek and deep wrinkles across my forehead, and he still told me I looked gorgeous. And trust me when I say … if I can do it, you can do it.

Thursday's date was a success even though I showed up as the mental illness patient that I am, I showed up with more uncertainty than what I thought I could handle, and I showed up with a life that has plenty of shattered parts. And despite those flaws, I laughed. He laughed. We had a pretty perfect time that Thursday night with our imperfect selves and a pretty perfect embrace to finish off the night.

Vulnerability does NOT equal shame. Shame is that voice inside our heads that tells us we're not good enough, pretty enough, smart enough, talented enough, etc. When you're vulnerable, you take risks and, according to Brown, those risks are the birthplace of creativity and innovation.

So the "I am bad/unworthy/not good enough" feeling associated with vulnerability is false; it's a F.E.A.R.–based thought that produces a negative self-image. The "I am bad/unworthy/not good enough" belief comes from secrecy, silence and judgment that grows when you do something that causes disappointment, like an eating disorder lapse, for instance.

It all boils down to the unreal expectation of women in today's age: do it all, do it perfectly, and never let 'em see you sweat. And ladies …

we just can't live that way. We have to take risks without emotions (yikes), we can't be afraid of being exposed for who we are and the story we have to tell, and we can't refrain from the uncertainty of life—good things are there waiting for our discovery. They are so very gray, and they're there for the taking. You just have to know up front that those things, which come from vulnerability, won't always be pretty.

And next, not three hours after leaving treatment … I lapsed.

With list in hand and focus on point, I made it through a grocery store errand in just over 30 minutes and headed home for the afternoon. I'd also purchased food according to my pre-planned lunch and dinner, and a couple extras made it into my cart as well.

I toasted two pieces of potato rosemary bread, scrambled two organic, cage-free eggs and tossed three pieces of organic, uncured bacon into the microwave. I like breakfast for meals other than breakfast—it's generally easy and gets the job done. Who doesn't like breakfast food, anyway?!

All my groceries were put away and I heard voices coming from the freezer and refrigerator. It was my eating disorder, calling on me to eat the "gray area" food that was now available to me, no longer at the store and out of reach.

*Nah, I don't need any of this food right now. I'm full and I've completed my planned lunch. I may eat some of this food later on, but not right now.*

Now experimenting with the introduction of dairy back into my diet, I tried some Gouda cheese new to the market from a major manufacturer. It is cut into small pieces, making it a convenient, easy snack.

Next thing I knew, the cheese had joined me on the couch.

I'd also bought a box of snack crackers to keep in my desk at work. I'd purposefully kept the two boxes of crackers in the grocery bag as a reminder to avoid over-grazing and to save them for snacks at work.

Abruptly, my willpower left the building. As if I'd completely lost control over my own decision-making, I broke into the box, eager to try the crackers, which were also new to the market and to me.

*You don't need these crackers! Especially after the cheese! Leave the box in the grocery bag; wait to have the crackers next week at work. Don't get them, Holly. Don't open the box … don't open the bag…*

But my voice wasn't loud enough. My eating disorder spoke and I listened. I gave in to its demands to eat the gray-area food.

I felt full, well beyond full. My stomach hurt. I felt control slip away in quiet tiny footsteps as if I wouldn't hear it leaving. I kept eating the crackers, in the pattern of one cracker per bite, two crackers per bite, and then three crackers per bite. I don't know why, but I've ended grazing binges on three items per bite. I don't know what it is about "three" that seems like the perfect end to a grazing binge. Would three crackers be more perfect than one or two? No. Would three satisfy me as the last bite more than one or two would? No. Would three be the number it would take for me to comfortably end my binge at that time? No.

The crackers went from tasty, yet just a tad too salty for my preference … to tasteless. I no longer savored the food. I only felt the food filling up my stuffed stomach, tearing away at my digestive system, getting into my head and drilling in guilt from believing that I'd done something bad.

*PUT THEM AWAY! Stop! There is no point in eating these crackers. You're not even hungry. They're meant for work. You've had enough to eat right now. You're going to be mad at yourself. You're going to feel tempted to isolate because of the shame binge eating brings you. Stop it, Holly! Stop all of it! You're too strong for this. You're too smart for this. You're on such a good track. Don't ruin it. Don't let this become something bigger than what it is right now.*

It was a lapse. And it was a lapse that I was able to end, but not without guilt, horrendous stomach pain and the reminder that I am very, very fragile. Most importantly, the lapse was possibly a blessing in disguise—just enough to take me off my high horse and remind me what took me to the EDTC in the first place … less than one month ago: to get help.

# CHAPTER 16

# Day 13
## *Monday, August 21*

Have you ever had a remarkably good day, and it was just that good for no reason in particular?

That was Monday's tune.

Even though I arrived that morning to an office where the air conditioning wasn't working during the mid–August heat wave, a circumstance that would have especially provoked my anxiety, it was like I had an inner spirit to keep me cool.

Ironically, it was the day of the solar eclipse and the once-in-a-lifetime event was set to peak in the Cincinnati region at about 2:30 p.m. I went to lunch with my friend from work, Alan, and I was grateful for the bonding experience with him. He's one of those walking encyclopedias. No matter how simple a question I ask him while at work, his answer lasts several minutes, at least!

From lunch, Alan and I walked a few blocks to Cincinnati's vibrant Washington Park. We caught some looks at the eclipse, but only through eyeglasses made especially to provide safe viewing of the sun. The weather was perfectly warm and bright, the park was packed, and we had a great midday outing before finishing up the day's duties.

The upbeat vibe came with me to the EDTC, and seeing one of the patients, Patrick, smile when I first walked only added to the cheer. Patrick has mentioned more than once that he struggles with confidence and loneliness, and I just don't see how he can feel that way (that's me on the outside looking in, of course). He's tall, and he sure is dark and handsome. His tan skin and black hair, paired with his adorable smile and smooth character ... I told my mom a few weekends ago that with

Patrick entering his freshman year of college, he'd have no problem with the ladies!

While my mood was up and anxiety was down, I still was in no place to get ticked off by another EDTC policy or value that could hit me the wrong way at any time. I asked Patrick and Sophia, who were both in the waiting area, if I'd be allowed to fill up my Nalgene water bottle in the water fountain just outside the lobby. I didn't want to take any chances; I didn't want to risk getting told "no," because I didn't want to come down from my natural, don't-look-a-gift-horse-in-the-mouth high.

Gladly, filling up the water bottle was cool ... and so therefore ... so was I.

My numbers at check-in made for my best report yet. Anxiety was a 5, irritability a 3 and mood an 8. I said that Saturday's group discussion really hit home, and that by thinking of my eating disorder as a future-oriented concept, I was able to better wrap my head around my need for treatment in the long run, since my eating disorder had seemed so dormant the last few weeks.

I didn't say this next part out loud to the group. Even though I'm 12 treatments in, there's a clear discomfort I have in admitting my lows to a room of acquaintances ... people who hardly know anything about me. Perhaps it's fear of exposure—a vulnerability battle that seems to be a repeated theme here. Maybe I think there's some type of way I'm SUPPOSED to appear for these people, to show up as someone who, because I'm a little older, more educated and more well rounded, feels a need to set a good example. I realize that I have a desire to be liked and to make friends, and maybe I even have a strong need for acceptance. I can also say that this group therapy is putting all this to the ultimate test.

The part that I just couldn't make known was my lapse from Saturday afternoon. *Aren't I too far along to feel that uncontrollable NEED for food? Aren't I smarter and stronger than that? Aren't I better than that? Everyone will think poorly of me if they know I made a mistake. I'll feel weak, ugly and desperate. Better keep the lapse to myself. I know I'll have to hear it from Isabella in my next meeting, anyway. That'll be enough.*

I scribbled on my check-in sheet, verbatim: "I'm kinda glad I had a small lapse. It was a good reminder that I'm not out of the woods yet."

As the group check-in session gave each patient the floor, I learned that one of my peers, Sophia, had relapsed. I do not know what eating disorder behaviors Sophia fights, but I could tell she'd returned to a very painful place. Her big, beautiful dark eyes were glossed over and swollen, and they were lined with a distinct red from unfortunate, regretful tears. Sophia had been friendly to me since I first met her and she enthusiastically lent me her phone charger. Because she once helped me out, I wanted to help her out. But I couldn't. I didn't understand her struggles, but I wanted so badly to take them from her. I wanted her struggles to no longer hurt her. Sophia doesn't deserve it, I thought with sympathy travelling from my heart to hers. In her check-in, Sophia asked to be left alone instead of being open to support. I wanted to do as she wished, but felt a desire to comfort her breaking out of my soul's confinement. I wanted to run over to Sophia, hold her, and tell her it was going to be OK.

The end of check-in transitioned into a video from Dove, "Beauty Is a State of Mind." Whatever you're doing right now, take a break and watch this video. Place a bookmark on this page, put down this book, and spend seven minutes watching the clip on YouTube.

It's jam-packed with empowerment (no spoiler alerts in this book). The video allows women to realize that if they felt a certain amount of confidence, that they didn't know they had, then they'd feel a new sense of ability to achieve greatness—and it all comes from … (*no spoiler alerts—you'll have to watch for yourself!*). Beauty isn't about the way you appear. Beauty is the ability to do things for yourself with no hesitation based on how you presume you look on the outside. That confidence might mean being able to approach a date, robustly lead your children, experience pure peace, break out of isolation, and even if it's the first time ever, feel comfortable in YOUR own skin. Now, try THAT on for size!

So you've likely heard this phrase like a million times: comfortable in your own skin. But what does comfortable in your own skin really mean? I'd always associated being comfortable in your own skin with being confident in who you are—in the present moment—with no desire to change or improve. When you're comfortable in your own skin, you're confident in the "as is" version of you.

I turned to body language expert Blanca Cobb, who told a Charlotte,

N.C., news station in 2016 that confidence is a lifestyle. It takes more than believing in yourself. You have to put confidence into action.

"You have to live it," Cobb said. "You can't just pull it out when you need it, you have to practice it all along."

Being confident, she says, is about being assertive and doing what's right regardless of what anybody else says. You need compassion for other people, but you need it for yourself too.

Without compassion, you can't have confidence because it's blocked by worry that you made a mistake, hurt someone's feelings or dropped a ball.

Confidence requires persistence.

"No matter when you're having self-doubt, you're still going to persist until you cross that finish line," Cobb said.

Confidence has to always be in your backpack if you plan on conquering the world ... or, OK, achieving your small goals too.

"Life is as beautiful as it is ugly, but when you're confident, you're going to be able to take calculated risks. You're going to be able to pave the path for yourself in what's going to make you happy."

For me, this meant being confident with every meal I ate, and putting my eating disorder behind me, one plate at a time. I know that one day I want to be free of my eating disorder, and while I may never be cured, I can choose to take risks with my eating.

*I can eat a slice of pizza without being triggered to devour the entire pie. I can eat a scoop of ice cream without wanting to put away a whole pint. I can be in front of a selection of food and put very little thought into my choice without feeling a drop of anxiety. I won't feel like an ugly girl at a dinner table of friends, where everyone else is eating a salad while I enjoy a juicy burger.* **My path to happiness is working to become completely comfortable in my own skin, especially when it comes to food.**

Dinnertime came after the Dove video and the engaging discussion. The video really seemed to move all of us.

A meal of turkey, mashed potatoes and cooked green beans was served Monday, but cold, raw baby carrots were offered as my veggie of choice. I'd eaten that meal before at the EDTC and didn't have too much hesitation. It wasn't my favorite, but taste-wise, it wouldn't be a struggle. Oddly, the mashed potatoes tasted terrible! They were way, way too salty and seasoned with garlic, and the metallic flavor felt like it could burn a hole in my tongue.

I finished eating all of the turkey and baby carrots on my plate, except for one carrot that had a brown end. I wanted the nutrition. I wanted to put nutrients and good stuff into my body to provide nourishment and strength, so I took one more bite of the potatoes. And no, not happening.

I asked Scarlet for a fruit-flavored Boost instead. I caught the EDTC-designed "second chance" lecture, which basically makes you feel like a slight failure for not completing the meal and so you have a "second chance" to eat a full dinner by supplementing the food with a Boost. I was also pleased when Scarlet told me that the fact that I actually wanted the Boost was a very good thing. The Boost drink is not served as punishment for incompletion of a meal; instead, it's a way to achieve success at dinner, by being the key that completes your required nutrition intake.

Have you ever eaten a big meal and felt really full? I'm going to assume we've all been there. So let's get clear on something: There's a difference in feeling uncomfortably full when you have an eating disorder and when you don't have the mental condition.

An eating disorder's version of uncomfortably full means much more than a stuffed belly. It's deeper. Fullness is falsely associated with guilt and disgust. After a full meal, people with an eating disorder will likely feel like they've done something wrong, they've broken a rule, and possibly the hardest part to swallow, they've let themselves down.

The disappointment can be the hardest reaction to bear for people with an eating disorder. They're overcome with remorse and they wish they could turn back the hands of time and handle the meal differently. They feel ugly and repulsive, as if the food that's now on the inside has the power to change what people see on the outside.

People who are not mentally ill with an eating disorder take comfort in knowing that although their belly feels chockful of food, the feeling will eventually go away once the food passes through their digestive system. It's nothing they become fixated on because they know it's a temporary feeling with no permanent impact.

People without an eating disorder don't attach themselves to the fullness like people with an eating disorder do. They are not gripped by chains of pain, which can wrap around the body, mind and soul like a hungry anaconda. People without an eating disorder can simply and effortlessly adopt acceptance that the full feeling will go away, just fizzle out in a short period of time.

The EDTC uses a treatment process of eating scheduled amounts of food with particular contents. Each time a patient eats a scheduled meal's contents, it's a step closer to fear of that overfilled feeling.

But also aligned with the EDTC's beliefs is that repeatedly over time, inching closer to that fear until you accept it and eventually knowing that you're going to be OK in its presence, is a mechanism to get you into recovery and further away from the chance of a relapse. You might never fully get over your eating disorder, but with treatment and work, you'll be able to experience fullness without attaching any meaning to the way your body feels after consuming a meal.

## CHAPTER 17

# Day 14

### *Wednesday, August 23*

They say it ain't over 'til the fat lady sings, so when I heard on Wednesday that she'd picked up the microphone, I wasn't at all ready for my final song.

Immediately before Wednesday's treatment session, I met with my therapist, Carmen. Carmen told me that although Mallory, the assessment specialist, had recommended six to eight weeks of treatment, she believed I was "just about ready to be on my way" after only four weeks.

Six weeks of treatment would have included 18 treatment sessions; eight weeks would have included 24. That Wednesday, I had only 14.

Carmen also said that since she reported my significant progress to my health insurance carrier, she highly doubted they'd cover additional sessions, even if I wanted to finish my original term.

I should have felt proud of myself for speeding through treatment and finding a place of recovery so much more quickly than expected, but instead, I felt like I'd come up short of maximizing my experience with the eating disorder treatment. What would I miss by not attending as many treatment sessions as originally planned?

Carmen suggested that my last day take place after three more treatments, which would have put us at Wednesday, August 30. I told Carmen that I would be unavailable that coming Saturday, so then we looked at a finish line of Saturday, September 2. But that's Labor Day weekend, and I doubted I'd be able to attend treatment due to plans during the holiday weekend.

No final treatment date was determined during my meeting with Carmen, but I knew it was coming close … too close for comfort.

*But I don't feel ready yet!* I told Carmen I was scared that I'd be released too soon, without the tools needed for if/when my eating disorder returned ... or *tried* to return. What would happen if I did fall back down into a pit of depression and turned to food for help instead of friends, family and healthy support?

Carmen reminded me that post-treatment is just as important as my three-times-weekly treatment sessions at the EDTC. In fact, post-treatment work has great potential to be more powerful because it requires serious solo effort, more self-accountability and more commitment, but all practiced with less support.

"That's when you really DO the work," Carmen said, "when you're no longer spending 12 hours per week at the EDTC and instead you're meeting with a therapist for one hour per week."

When I'm back out on my own, I'll really be put to the test. I'll no longer have check-ins multiple times per week, so I'll have to monitor my behavior with an independent system. The education I receive three times per week will also come to a halt, and I'll have to use what's in my backpack to guide the way. I'll be solely responsible for all meals I consume, without those that the EDTC provided three times a week.

I might stumble upon difficult decisions and I'll have to rely on my own judgment to make healthy choices. I will be triggered by things in my environments, and I'll have to stand strong, unaffected by them. I'll gain 12 hours each week that will open many doors for how I spend my time, and I'll need to dedicate that time to something that will benefit my progress and support my well-being.

I won't be free and I won't be fixed. I'll be on a path forward—a path into the unknown—a path that will come with lessons to learn, because there is no "end" to living with an eating disorder.

*How can I possibly feel confident when taking that next step? I haven't yet achieved my original three goals from my therapy with Carmen: to normalize eating behaviors, to get more comfortable in gray areas of life, and to end all black-and-white thinking. I'm still not OK. I'm not sure I can make good decisions on my own, without the reminders that I take away from each treatment session. What if I fail? What if I end up on my couch in tears again? What if I mess up with too many meals and I can't straighten myself out? What if new friendships don't work out? What if the stress of my eating disorder goes with me to work? What if everything falls apart? What if I'm never able to experience being in the clear?*

It didn't seem fair.

*Do the EDTC therapists want to discharge me because no one likes me?*

*Stop it, Holly. You know damn well that's not the case. They want the best for you. They're pleased with your work. They're happy with your progress. And you should be too. STOP waiting to feel "perfect" and stop focusing on being "fixed." Realize your recovery is a gray area and be there—in the thick of it—because this is life and you have to live every day with an open mind.*

**I will look forward. I will look forward.**

When I first learned about Wednesday evening's exercise, it sounded anything but appealing. It seemed like a waste of time—something that wouldn't produce results of strong, unforgettable lessons that I could use moving forward. I had a shaper eye than normal on Wednesday because I knew the end of treatment was near, and I wanted to pack each session with as much engagement and power as possible.

First came a handout, then came about 30 food magazines. We selected a magazine or two and used its contents to complete the assignment: Find four nutrition claims and decide if they're fact or fiction. Next, find a surprising food fact based on discussions and promotions found in the magazine. Last, using the recipes inside, find a day's worth of meals and snacks that will work with our meal plans.

The exercise felt too close to arts and crafts, and not close enough to solid, legit education. I'd rather sit in a classroom and hear a lecture on something that can truly help me get better than to look through food magazines and discuss what we found. Only with my stubborn ways tossed to the side did I become present and able to participate.

Once I mentally pushed myself into the exercise, it was quite eye opening to see the kind of material included in ads and promos, and even more—how can they get away with such wording?

So many ads base their claims on research, but they never cite the study. A food manufacturer can claim its products are healthier because "a percentage" of "some test group or some set of people" say so. But who are these research participants, when was the research done and where can readers find evidence of the analysis? That's Journalism 101—all research findings must be properly cited.

Next, I came across a page that made me gasp so loud that my peers looked up from their own magazine scanning to see what my reaction was all about. An ad for a new app, which allows users an all-access pass to numerous online magazines, used a very disturbing marketing message: "Binge reading. It's about to be a thing."

*Binge reading. In a magazine about food. In a place where people with eating disorders are exposed to messages … and are hyper-sensitive to them too. Binge reading. Someone who suffers from binge eating (me) is actually holding the magazine in which the message is printed and reading its very words. Binge reading. Binge eating. Have you lost your damn mind?*

I couldn't describe the direct impact, if any, the ad had on my mentality. But I found myself with a slew of "what if" questions and wondering how the ad might affect others. What if the ad triggered someone to have a binge-eating episode? What if the ad hit someone with an eating disorder hard enough to make them feel significantly self-conscious or even dig up old depression? What if the ad made someone's depressive state worse? What if the ad triggered a binge eater to binge eat?

And who's to blame: the magazine company for approving the ad, or the marketers who created the ad's message? Regardless, someone missed some serious consideration when this ad made it to print and from there hit store shelves and finally landed in the hands of readers. Someone dropped the ball. Big time.

The third ad I noted surprisingly allowed me to see a popular health trend very differently—a trend that millions have followed in recent years. The buzz of clean eating is irrefutably loud and popular vote says the best way to go is with simple ingredients and the fewer, the better.

It's a widely-known fact: You need four ingredients to make a loaf of bread, including flour, salt, yeast and water. The additives, like artificial preservatives and high fructose corn syrup that's found in major bread brands, are certainly not needed.

So yes, in many cases, fewer ingredients is a good thing when it comes to healthy eating.

However, when I saw an ad for a cream cheese that read, "Our ingredient list is shorter than their ingredient list. Simply better," I had a change of heart, which I fully attribute to the EDTC's philosophies on nutrition, because without the teachings of the EDTC, I would have bought into this ad, literally.

If there are fewer ingredients in food, the manufacturer might be able to say its product is simpler than competitors' products. But is the simple version of the food missing out on important nutrition, all because the additive ingredients that contain key vitamins and minerals have been removed to appeal to the clean eating trend followers?

And what's more important: providing nutritious food or using diet trends to increase sales?

Manufacturers, if you can think this question through and answer with the latter option, then we have a big problem.

And here's another one to throw out there: Let's say a manufacturer of a beauty product offers an anti-aging cream. What does anti-aging even mean? In all reality, anti-aging could mean the ability to stop becoming older and increase the number of years that describes our age. As beauty-conscious consumers, the term "anti-aging" has sadly become defined by the ability to reduce signs of aging that show up on our face as we grow older, like wrinkles, crow's feet and loss of elasticity.

Women: Be empowered to question these messages and detach from their claims. A product cannot stop the clock; it cannot "anti-age" you. Sometime this year, your age will increase by one year, regardless if you do, or do not use, an "anti-aging" skin care product. Happy birthday in advance.

Moral of the story, coming from someone with an eating disorder and a journalism background: Read every word of the ad, see if its contents align with your values, and see what evidence (if any) is out there to back the ad's claim. Messages that seem like a good idea, unbiased and fair, and even inspirational, may only cause you to waste time and money. Instead, they might only be the manufacturer's best bet for increased revenue.

Dinner was easy come, easy go. Breaded chicken filets, diced potatoes in olive oil and seasoning, and cooked vegetables (raw carrots for me) were served. The food tasted as good as the first time it was offered, only the chicken tasted a bit more fresh and the olive oil was a bit on the side of too heavy. Nonetheless, I ate everything on my plate while small talk with EDTC peers filled dinnertime's allotted 30 minutes.

Sparked by discussion on current pop culture, I realized that it's difficult to carry on meaningful conversation with others at the EDTC. We all know we have something in common—obviously an eating disorder—but we don't know which type of disorder each other has, and we don't know any detail of each others' struggles. There's an age gap between my peers and myself, and I often don't know what to talk about. The majority of my peers are in college, and I find myself trying to recollect my college days so that I can better relate to them, but that was well over a decade ago.

What were the big things going on back in college? What did I do for fun? What stressed me out? What did my college friends and I talk about back in those days? My memory always seemed like a blur from what was actually a very significant time in my life, but for some reason, I still felt disconnected from my peers.

*But people who you might find hard to relate to could most certainly be your biggest support system. Try, Holly, try. Look deep. Look beyond age. Look beyond your bullshit ego. Embrace these people. You deserve them. You need them.*

And so I did. After dinner, I unapologetically used Process time to talk about my gray area pressure, to open up to my peers, and see what new ideas and understandings I could walk away with. I truly felt their insight could become a valuable

A 2006 graduate of the University of Kentucky's College of Agriculture, I returned to Lexington to walk in the spring commencement ceremony at Rupp Arena in May 2007.

tool to help fight any future temptations that would toss me back into disordered eating habits.

"So my struggle comes from black-and-white thinking," I started speaking to the group, "and as I've just learned that my time with the EDTC is shortly ending, I want to use this time to learn how I can cope once I'm out. Right now, my eating disorder is dormant and because life has been more motivating and fulfilling outside of treatment, I don't feel strongly aligned with eating disorder behaviors.

"And because I know my eating disorder is triggered by loneliness, anxiety and lack of excitement to look forward to, how do I enter into those triggers and be OK when they make my life gray? It's inevitable that my depression ebbs and flows, so how do I approach the next decline with an allowance for a gray area and without the expectation that life has to be perfect? I either eat in a way that's really good, or a way that's really bad."

I continued to unleash my emotions, revealing more details about my beliefs and insecurities than I ever thought I would.

"That goes for relationships too," I said. "When a friend lets me down or upsets me, how do I live with a gray-area friendship? If a friend doesn't call, they're too rarely available, they make me feel like I'm replaced by another friend, or it seems like they're all talk and no action (real scenarios), it's so hard to drop expectations and embrace the friends that they truly are. I believe they care about me, but they're comfortably living in gray and I'm not; they're probably unaware that there's even a problem, likely because I created it and kept it inside. It's even more difficult to confront those friends and to let them know I'm a bit disappointed. And I don't know why it's difficult. It's just one conversation, right?

"That also goes for self-acceptance. Since I'm a black-and-white thinker, you can imagine what that means when it comes to my appearance and the time I spend trying to get 'up to my beauty standard.' For me, there's no gray area when it comes to looks and beauty, so I've spent a lot of time and money (too much time and money) trying to 'fix' things. No wonder I've been through more than 20 medical corrective procedures, some surgeries, to fix my acne scars. And no wonder I'm still not happy because some of them are still there—laid out on my cheeks, and my skin texture looks like a gravel driveway in certain light.

"And that perfection rules my practices at home too. My linen closet is perfectly organized, and a junk drawer doesn't exist. And yes, that's a thing to a black-and-white thinker. A house isn't clean unless it's spotless from top to bottom."

And then I took my soapbox to an unbelievably personal, private place.

"Generally, in my way of thinking, a state of good enough doesn't exist because of pressure to be the best I can be. So my F.E.A.R.-based thought is that everyone else sees me as not good enough, because while I'm (falsely) aware of any room for improvement—even in the tiniest millimeter or millisecond or milliunit—I don't think I'm good enough.

"So how can anyone possibly fully accept and love me if I can't fully accept and love myself?"

Here's what I took away Wednesday night, thanks not only to one of my favorite EDTC therapists, Phoebe, but to the handful of insightful, kind peers who were there:

An eating disorder separates you from your values. My eating disorder separates me from balance, optimal health and control. When I'm hit with a binge-eating episode, in that moment, I'm instantly willing to lose balance, to sacrifice my health, and I can't maintain control despite the crucial need for power.

A conflict over food is like a squirrel in the country's busiest intersection. *What do I do? Which way do I go? Where do I turn? I'm gonna get run over! I might cause a wreck! Oh no!*

With practice over time, and especially soon after treatment, I'll work on stopping to acknowledge times when my values are pulled away by eating disorder urges. By simply stopping and allowing the urge to exist, you can confront it head on. You can fight it. You can become stronger than the urge. You can win.

You can refuse to lose balance, you can make the healthy choice and hold onto control.

With all areas—food, relationships, beauty, etc.—the gray area's not going to be pretty. It's going to be uncomfortable because it's sloppy and you'll be exposed to vulnerability. More often than not, black-and-white thinkers cannot bear the discomfort. Instead, a perfectionist doesn't sit with the exposure, and he or she does anything in his or her power to correct what he or she sees as a problem. It's a strategy that's proven to work for black-and-white thinkers: They find a reliable theory that typically takes away exposure by fixing, improving, or enhancing the discomfort's root cause, until it reaches a suitable state, which, usually, in the eye of a perfectionist, is a state of flat-out perfection ... because not until then is the condition good enough.

The EDTC uses a linear model called Radically Open Dialectical Behavior Therapy (RO-DBT), which shows that some patients are under controlled, and some are overly controlled. Those who under control are prone to binge eating, and those who over control will likely suffer from anorexia nervosa. My condition is not typical as it contradicts this model, which means I'd need to take on over-controlled coping techniques.

That starts with self-inquiry. Self-inquiry is a technique in which you ask yourself questions not to necessarily get answers or solve problems, but to open doors to what's possible.

Self-inquiry questions help you discover what possibilities are available to help you, though you might not find an answer. Self-inquiry is not a guarantee for a solution, nor is that the goal. The process of self-inquiry reaps more benefit than the result and provides the possibility of realizing you're OK in a given moment, gaining some comfort and then asking, "OK, now what?!"

Where did I get the idea that foods are "good" or "bad"?
Where did I first find that idea?
Where do my judgments come from?
Why don't I think I can break away from those judgments?
Where would that freedom take me?
What would the release feel like?

As you uncover more and more questions, the self-inquiry practice works with you. The continued work of self-inquiry draws new awareness, and it promotes healing and growth.

# CHAPTER 18

# Day 15

## *Monday, August 28*

I skipped treatment again on Saturday, August 26, but for a different reason than just not wanting to go. That was the morning of an annual yoga event that I'd attended every year since moving to Cincinnati, and I didn't want to miss it. It's a special practice held on Great American Ball Park, home of the Cincinnati Reds. Sun salutations, handstands and arm balances in center field were a must.

Regretfully, plans for the yoga event fell through just before time to arrive at the ballpark, but I quickly had replacement plans to fill Saturday morning—time with a new friend, which was so on cue with fulfillment that I needed and so desperately wanted in my quest to become "good enough" for friends.

We took a mid-morning fitness class together and then met a handful of her friends for brunch at a nearby Italian restaurant. While at brunch, I was careful to order a meal that would provide an ideal amount of nutrition, fully aware that the practice of careful meal consideration would soon become my reality as I got closer to the end of treatment.

I had two pieces of bread dipped in herbed olive oil, a common appetizer at Italian restaurants. My meal was a mixed field greens and Caprese salad topped with salmon. It was delicious, satisfying and very EDTC–approved as it provided the recommended macronutrients.

After finishing our meals, we parted ways for the afternoon, but later met back up for a German festival in a neighborhood on the northwest edge of Cincinnati. I enjoyed a tall Oktoberfest beer while hanging with a group of new faces. The brew complemented the warm summer evening nicely.

I grew fearful of dinner while walking around the festival. I was doing plenty of people watching, but I was also doing plenty of food watching … or lack thereof. I felt my anxiety climb, and with a narrow selection of food to choose from for dinner, I severely worried about what I would eat and if it would fill the need for nutrition. *I hope no one noticed how uneasy I was for part of Saturday evening, as worry is typically written all over my face.* I ate a German Mettwurst and part of a Bavarian pretzel. I opted out of eating the greasy, fried potato pancakes, which I didn't believe I could stomach. I don't even think vegetables were served at the festival, or at least I didn't see any.

Saturday night's dinner raised a solid question: *The Mettwurst and pretzel did not meet nutrition requirements for a meal, so obviously it would be unacceptable in the EDTC's perspective. But if I'm supposed to be OK with gray-area eating, how should I handle the less-than-perfect dinner? How should I react to eating a meal that didn't satisfy nutrition requirements, but be OK with the fact that it was my only option AND that it was far from satisfactory? What should I do in that situation, because it wasn't the first time in a setting with limited nutrition, and I doubt it will be my last?*

I got home at about 11 p.m., and I considered eating a handful of kale, just to get in the evening's missed vegetable, but I didn't want to wake up with a stomachache either. So I went to bed with the plan to make up for lost nutrition Sunday morning, and after waking up, I followed through with TWO servings of vegetables (two huge handfuls of spinach) as part of a green protein smoothie I made myself. There. Maybe that's best.

Monday's treatment session opened with an exercise on body image, which included a little research. We were each given 10 pieces of paper. Each piece pictured a woman who represented a body ideal for her era, and the body ideal went hand in hand with the fashion each woman wore. From there, we ordered the photos according to which decade we thought each one came from: 1910 through the 2000s.

Patrick was my partner in the exercise. He'd actually completed the exercise in a previous treatment before my time at the EDTC, so he took the driver's seat and nailed it!

Since 1910, body ideals have been all over the place, with major shifts in what was considered "ideal" from decade to decade. In each 10-year period, a different body type served as a goal for women—an aspiration to look a certain way—all to meet social expectations created by models and print media.

According to Nina Bahadur, a deputy editor at *Huffington Post*, body ideals from decade to decade symbolized women's roles in each era.

"A woman with a 'perfect body' in 1930 would barely get a second look from Hollywood producers or model casting agents today," she wrote in 2014.

"Looking back on the 'ideal' women throughout the past century tells us just how arbitrary any version of 'the perfect body' is," Bahadur said. "Sex symbols have varied in terms of body shape, weight, height and tone."

**1900–1910s:** The ideal figure was tall with a large bust and wide hips, and a narrow waist. She was seen everywhere from the theater, to the church, to working at the upscale department store.

**1920s:** Flappers in this era wore bobbed hair and shorter dresses, and they took on more outrageous, perhaps immoral, conduct like smoking in public and getting behind the wheel. Flappers drew less attention to their breasts and waists than the earlier ideals and instead showed their ankles or knees.

**1930s:** Figures were once again flaunted in this decade, with tight-fitting attire that highlighted the waist and hips.

**1940s:** The 1920s ideals were seen again in this era, when such curves as boasted in the 1930s were now unattainable. The 1940s reintroduced the Flapper-like free-spirited dress, slender but healthy body.

**1950s:** In this decade, bodies were "meant to be seen," as Marilyn Monroe once said. Women showed as much of their bodies as they could get away with—flaunting long legs and busty, hourglass figures.

**1960s:** A never-seen-before ideal hit the 1960s along with the sexual revolution. Women revealed their slim, long legs and very small frames—the ideal body was skinnier than ever before. Dress moved from the tight, form-fitting style to one that concealed a woman's size, even if she was very thin.

**1970s:** Athletics formed the ideal body in the 70s, but also marked the decade was the rise of anorexia nervosa because women desperately wanted to be thin. On one hand, women were tan with long hair and toned, muscular bodies. On the other, more and more women avoided food to maintain low weight and eating disorders went through the roof.

**1980s:** "Hardbodies" took over the 80s as the athletic body type became more attractive. Thin may have been good, but strong was better. The desire to be thin faded out in the 80s as the fitness fad set the tone for the new ideal. It was all about being tall, in excellent shape and having built muscles.

**1990s:** In this decade, extremely thin figures once again became the ideal. Women moved from the gym to the place where visible bone structure, scrawny limbs and pale skin reigned supreme.

**2000s:** The 21st century rounded up some ideals from past decades and created a new look. Tall, thin and leggy stayed around, and so did a full chest and muscle tone. The ideal body was in shape, healthy and proud. And it was attainable. Realistic.

**2010s:** And here we are in a new world where women feel empowered to do away with body ideals and find comfort being themselves—in all shapes and sizes.

But quite to the contrary, we see a rise in plastic surgery today—women willing to pay thousands and undergo operations to obtain an image that they see as ideal and wish to make theirs. It's like women have become obsessed with the idea of "fixing" their flaws, perhaps too small to even be seen by others.

While more of a variety of ideals exist today—perhaps more than ever before—women will go to excessive lengths to achieve greatness, as they see from the outside.

Dinner was a fiasco despite what the dry-erase board said. I read that dinner would include a wheat roll and butter, a mixed green house-style salad and chicken Alfredo pasta. Thinking back to the salad dressing disaster that happened when this meal was served a couple weeks before, I remembered the chicken and pasta combo served that night was very tasty. I was pleased to eat it once more.

I grabbed a roll and a packet of butter. Next, I once again came up on a salad ... and the forever-dreaded, never-happening Ranch dressing. I loaded a serving of salad onto my plate and nonchalantly passed the dressing and Susie stopped me, dead in my tracks.

*Great (I'm positive that I rolled my eyes and snarled the left side of my top lip). Here we go. No Ranch for this girl. Get out of my way. Leave me alone. Let me eat my dinner without conflict so that I can actually enjoy what's being served.*

I was ready to put my foot down this time. *We've had the salad dressing discussion. We don't need to have it once again. I'm NOT eating the Ranch. Period. End of story.*

"The bread actually isn't in your meal plan," Susie said, observing my plate before catching eye contact with me.

I was startled for just a second, realizing the dressing hadn't been my downfall, but this time around, it was the dinner roll.

"But I touched it, so I can't put it back. Can I not just eat it? I'll just eat it," I said with a nonchalant shoulder shrug. No big deal, right? I really didn't think it would cause a catastrophe; the roll was barely the size of a baseball.

Lo and behold, Susie refused to let me keep the dinner roll, and I had to throw the bread into the garbage can. Once again, I looked out onto the crowded streets below and imagined the number of hungry people who would see the dinner roll as priceless bites of food—maybe even the only food they would get for the night. It took no time, and nothing further, for my anger to shoot through the roof and bust out the windows.

I instantly tried to let go of my rage and latch onto any tranquility and composure I could find.

**I will look forward. I will look forward.**

Looking back at the food selection, I saw the chicken Alfredo pasta and was eager to dig in. That was strike two! I put too much of the main course on my plate and was told to put some of it back.

"I'm going to have to eat when I get home because you are taking food away from me!" I asserted, with anger surge on repeat.

At that very point, I felt myself thrusting the plate of food against the countertop, so hard that it shattered into pieces of ceramic and food flew in every direction. In that moment, I recalled the scene in *The Devil*

*Wears Prada* when Miranda Priestly rejects Andy's delivery of a Smith & Wollensky's steak. Andy loses her cool after so much pressure from her boss, heads to the office's kitchen area and chucks the uneaten steak, plate and all, into a sink so the plate shatters and the meat is wasted in the mess.

Despite outrageous fury and the recollection of Priestly's Manhattan office, I managed to keep plate in hand. I took my seat and ate my meal, all while joining in conversation among my peers. I was determined to rise above the EDTC–induced dinner roll wrath and main course madness. So I sat there. And I sucked it up. And it ended up being OK.

I brought the dinner devastation to Process, desperately wanting answers to the confusion I'd just experienced.

"I'm feeling triggered in a way that I haven't been triggered since starting treatment," I said, specifically looking at the almighty Scarlet, with confidence she'd know just what to say to help me.

"I'm not full. I want more food. I want to go home and eat so that I'm satisfied, which makes a binge-eating episode very likely. I was told to throw part of my meal away, and then I was told to put back some of the meal because I added too much to my plate. Frustration is a trigger of my eating disorder and right now I don't feel good … not even a little bit. This doesn't make any sense to me at all. I'm so mad right now."

So Scarlet took my concern and began working her magic.

When someone is prescribed a medication, she said, she takes that medication according to doctor's orders. A certain, specific amount of medicine is needed to cure the illness—no more, no less. Scarlet said that for now, my dietician is my doctor and that my meal plan is the medicine. While the meal plan isn't used as a cure, it's used as a regimen to help me get on track with nutritious eating.

Also, as if it wasn't the most obvious solution to my dinner problem and lurking hunger…

"Just eat a snack," Scarlet said, with a tranquil "What's the big deal?" touch.

A snack! Simple as that.

A snack is so important, I learned, in ending cravings and prevention of overeating at meals. Going too long without any food is a direct route to an eating disorder's overpowering temptation.

Normal thinking, thinking unaffected and/or uninterrupted by an eating disorder's voice, is that you'd accept the meal for what it is, Scarlet said. Maybe it's not quite enough; maybe it's just a bit more than an ideal portion. Maybe it's unfulfilling and maybe it's unpleasant.

And so just eat a snack. That's it. A snack.

It's not rocket science.

Eating a snack is the easiest way to think less rigidly about a meal, Scarlet said. When you base eating on a meal plan, after time and practice, you learn to accept it, and you learn how to subtract thoughts and judgment from food, and...

WAIT, HOLD UP! Another voice chimed in from across the room...

Scarlet's always-helpful insight was interrupted by a peer named Bonnie, who in my opinion, really likes to hear herself talk. I didn't *want* to hear what Bonnie had to say or what she thought. I didn't *care* what she had to say. She's not a professional. Scarlet's the professional, and she's the one who can relate to me and speak to me and give me perspective that no one else can. When Scarlet provides help, it's absolutely priceless to me. It's the best. And so far, it had proven to be the biggest facilitator of my recovery.

So when Bonnie followed up Scarlet's guidance, it went from annoying to frustrating to infuriating all within just a few of Bonnie's not-so-helpful sentences.

In fact, it made me totally forget the advice Scarlet had just given me, which had made so much sense and had allowed me to see frustration from dinner in a whole new light—a light that brought new understanding and promoted my rational thinking, instead of fighting what seemed so unclear. I even broke the rules and grabbed my phone to try and record anything I could muster from what Scarlet had said. I made no eye contact with Bonnie. I tried so hard to block her out. I wanted her rambling to stop immediately. The more she carried on, the further away I got from Scarlet's helpful knowledge and leadership.

It was all I could do to keep myself in my seat. My breathing was fast and deep. My heartbeat made my chest quiver. A sharp pain slammed my forehead and temples. My fingernails grew sore and near bleeding from my picking and biting. I tried to swallow my own saliva and couldn't.

Get me out of here. Get me out of here NOW.

Ferocity got worse as Process went on. I have no idea what insight or what dinner experiences Ruth and Bonnie shared of their own during the remaining 45 minutes of Monday's session. Mentally, I was already in my car, well on my way home. I was screaming on the inside, angry that a peer's opinion stripped away helpful direction and feedback that I could use in my recovery. I want you to stop talking, Bonnie. Stop talking now. I don't believe that you're well informed to truly help me, and more than anything, I don't feel like what you have to say is genuine in the slightest. STOP talking.

*Should I walk out? I can't. They'll ask questions and I'll lose my cool. Should I excuse myself and just say, "I gotta go"? But what if they follow me? Would I need to dash to the stairwell and rush down four flights of stairs because they'll catch me waiting on the elevator? Maybe they'll physically grab me and not let me leave. Should I blame it on "work that just hit my inbox"? Maybe I could use my headache as an excuse to leave early. Look at the carpet. Look out the window. Maintain eye contact with Scarlet when she talks. She can calm me down. Don't make eye contact with your peers. They'll see the anger in your burning eyes. Sit there. Fold your hands in your lap. Don't move. Don't sigh too loud. Stay there. Stick it out. Commit. Take it. Handle it. Sit there with it. Don't leave, Holly, don't leave. Breathe. Slowly.*

Voices became nails on chalkboards—either I heard a soft-spoken, annoying mouse or I heard a masculine, scratchy tone that sounded like it was painful to speak. It was certainly painful to hear.

I actually felt my seat come an inch or two out of my chair when EDTC therapist Catherine asked for everyone around the room to say one thing they'd take home from Monday night's session. *Sit back down, Holly.*

"I'm taking home a headache," I said. "I don't want to be here anymore. I have a hard out at 8 p.m. and it's 8:01, and I'm really ready to go." I followed with a shoulder shrug and half-smile-turned-unapologetic smirk. *Yeah—it's a shitty answer, but right now, I don't care.*

It took every little ounce of strength I had to keep from an explosion, wherein I would snatch up my handbag and rush for the door, frantic to reach my car and be out of there, on my way home. And it wasn't until I arrived home, walked in my door and just sat still for a while that I was able to reach out and grab onto the evening's first sense of calm.

"SHUT UP! JUST SHUT UP!" I yelled out loud, to absolutely no one, so loud that my scream made my throat hurt just after those five words. The release felt good, if nothing else came from my solo outburst.

I noted at 8:56 that night that my breathing had finally slowed to a normal pace, and the beat of my heart had quieted.

And just how did Monday night end? With a protein shake and amino acids ... and ... an ENTIRE bag of dried cranberries.

# CHAPTER 19

# Day 16

## *Wednesday, August 30*

For the very first time, some of the answers I had been diligently searching for since learning that I would soon be discharged FINALLY emerged and started to become attainable at Wednesday's treatment session.

*Will judgment of food ever fade and eventually go away?*

*Will I ever stop wondering whether I made the right choice, meal to meal?*

*Will I ever be able to prepare and enjoy a meal without wanting more food?*

*How do I know my meal choice is based on what I want, instead of being based on what I want according to my eating disorder?*

Those answers were uncovered after the evening exercise and dinner, but I'll get to that part shortly.

Wednesday evening began with a group outing to the Whole Foods Market, located in the EDTC's adjacent shopping center. But I didn't go. I stayed inside the confidential, protective walls of the EDTC. Too afraid of running into someone I know, I could create the reality in my mind—there I am, in Whole Foods with a worksheet, completing exercises like naming a produce item that's a good source of Vitamin D, or listing an item that would count as a serving of fat, along with recording how much of that item you should consume in one sitting.

Being physically present in the notoriously popular grocery store, especially during the busy evening hours, definitely marked unsafe territory—what if I ran into a friend? An acquaintance? A familiar face from the tightly connected fitness and yoga community? Or the unthinkable—an ex-boyfriend? And what if they caught me red handed with pen and paper from an eating disorder treatment center, completing an assignment? I shuddered to think of how embarrassed I'd be, even though living with an eating disorder, or any mental health issue for that matter, is NOTHING (I repeat ... nothing) to be ashamed of. I just wasn't ready to risk sharing something that I'd kept secret for 15 years.

So I opted out, which to my surprise went over very well with EDTC staff. Using my smartphone and the fact that I know the layout of that Whole Foods like the back of my hand, I completed the worksheet from the comfort of the EDTC treatment room's couch. To be honest, I didn't get much out of the exercise, but I stayed engaged during the worksheet discussion to have compassion for my peers.

The assignment was a big learning opportunity for them, and I wanted support to leap from my soul and fill the room with encouragement and empowerment as we talked about what foods they found to complete the assignment and how all those foods can be a great fit for a balanced, nutrition-filled meal plan.

I must have been more absorbed by the discussion than I'd thought because suddenly, the 6:30 p.m. dinnertime arrived and we headed toward the cafeteria.

With ease instead of reluctance, I placed a cut of beef short rib, a cup of garlic mashed potatoes and 10 baby carrots (my usual go-to vegetable at the EDTC) on my plate. It was the second time we'd had that meal for dinner, and I remembered enjoying it the first time. However, this time, not so much. The meat had more fat along the top and throughout the cube-shaped cut.

I scraped the obvious slimy fat off the meat's surface and placed it toward the outer rim of my plate—careful it didn't make contact with the appetizing mashed potatoes and get-the-job-done raw carrots. Then, I finished my meal, but not without gagging a few times as I swallowed the fat-filled, slimy, lukewarm beef short rib. The five-year-old in me wanted to dunk each bite of meat into a pool of ketchup to disguise the terrible taste and texture, but unfortunately, the condiment would have been "against EDTC rules."

Meal Process began once we returned to the treatment room, and

I was relieved to hear the words of a newer patient, April, echo the exact thoughts I had about the meal. She said she noticed the fat hanging onto the meat and that she didn't want to eat that part. She too scraped off the fat and pushed it aside, but not without apprehension—almost an expectation—that the EDTC staff would say the fat counts as part of the meal and that, in fact, the meal wouldn't count as complete so long as the fat was left behind. April said she expected that she'd have to drink some of a Boost supplement because she'd planned to refuse the fat if, in fact, the debate came up.

I was relieved to hear the EDTC dietician Emma's response, and I'm pretty sure April was too. Emma said that the EDTC staff would never expect patients to eat something they wouldn't eat, meaning the fat removal was OK. It's one thing to scrape off the obvious fat but it's another to dig in with a microscopic eye, leaving no fat unturned. A certain sigh of relief for April and me.

Now let's get back to the start of Wednesday, the good stuff—the answers to my burning questions ... EVERYTHING I'd yet to find out.

*Judging food; choosing right or wrong foods; feeling satisfied; silencing conflicting thoughts about food: tell me what to do*! I was ready to start begging for things to finally make sense, considering the jump in my anxiety knowing my last day of treatment was right around the corner.

Let's start by talking about motivations associated with eating habits. Some are short-term, like the motivation to eat at least three or four servings of fruits or vegetables per day. Other motivations are long-term, like when in the future, eating three or four servings of vegetables becomes natural and unplanned, and there's no effort needed to do so.

Regardless of length, here's the key: Make sure all motivators are stronger than eating disorder urges and triggers. Make your will to eat healthy bigger and stronger than your urge to binge eat, regardless if this lasts for a portion of your day or if it lasts for months or even years.

Harper (not the same Harper from early chapters) is a newer peer to the Intensive Outpatient group. Harper stood out to me from the get-go, as her features demand attention and respect when she enters the room: black hair, porcelain skin, sharp, bold eyebrows and piercing eyes. Harper's in acting school at a Cincinnati university, and her beautiful expressions and tantalizing gestures make her future success in the theater exceptionally promising. Watch out, Hollywood.

Harper shared an analogy Wednesday evening that hit home with quite a few of us. She sees her eating disorder like a bank account. Each time she eats a Fear Food, she "spends money" in her bank account. So a food she thinks is fattening, triggering, or "bad" costs more than "good" foods that she thinks won't contribute to weight loss, eating disorder behaviors and guilt. Harper said that by the end of the day, she feels she cannot "afford" to eat certain foods, and that's she's "out of money." When you put it like that, it makes total sense that the bank account of someone with an eating disorder would be well on its way to an overdraft.

Up next was Phoebe's algebra analogy, the second concept to hit home that night. She recalled college-level algebra classes, during which she'd literally be brought to tears by big, complicated mathematics. The algebra problems she had to work out were so immense and complex, Phoebe said she didn't even know where to start. Eventually, and before the semester ended, Phoebe figured out what to do: Break the math problem down into smaller, more manageable parts.

Let's relate Phoebe's algebra strategy to the management of an eating disorder.

Quite literally, the immense, complex eating disorder brings you to tears. It's too big. You can't solve the equation. After some time and practice, you'll finally formulate a reliable strategy to make your eating disorder easier to manage. As with algebra, break your eating disorder down into manageable parts. Those parts will be the meals and snacks that make up the big calculation, a.k.a. your day of eating.

"When you can handle the parts, only then can you handle the whole," Phoebe said.

Genius!

Now, let's look at the upcoming end of Intensive Outpatient treatment. When a patient steps away from treatment and goes into the world, no longer equipped with three weekly EDTC sessions, it's very likely they'll feel more pressure, temptation, and they'll be apt to lose control at times, particularly at home.

Think of this new intensity as a challenge. And rise above it. Handle it. Like a boss.

What can you do to be in control?

The EDTC recommends distraction as a coping technique. When you feel triggered to binge or act out with eating disorder behaviors, do something to take your thoughts away from the food and the behavior. Take your thoughts elsewhere—to a place that has nothing to do with food. Spend some time there. Then, reevaluate how you feel about food and the craving you just experienced. Is it weaker? Is it gone?

I put distraction into action at home the following Friday evening. I'd had my planned meals and snacks for the day, and from a nutrition standpoint, I needed no more food to satisfy my day's quota. But I felt a pang. I felt a hunger—a false hunger.

So I vacuumed. I took 10 minutes to vacuum the first floor of my condo, and I even got some satisfaction from the freshly swept pattern left by the sweeper's tracks. Even though I'd just vacuumed a few days prior to that Friday, it felt so clean and refreshing!

And voila! My food craving was significantly tuned down. It wasn't gone, but it was quiet enough that I could carry on with my quiet evening at home without excessive eating.

Victory (if only for a day).

There had been plenty of occasions when I'd eaten healthy and made gray-area food choices to practice the feeling of freedom that I wanted so badly to feel regarding food. However, the first hint of depression and anxiety triggered my false desire to eat outside my meal plan. I felt tempted many times to blame my allowance of a minor binge on my quest for gray-area eating and to also use my practice of being in the gray area as an excuse for slipping up and eating according to my sneaky, eating disorder influence.

What beliefs are true when it comes to expectations for meal plans? How perfectly matched with a meal plan are you supposed to be? What if you get off track?

As if she didn't think twice about the simple solution, Phoebe said it's all about dropping every expectation and allowing for flexibility and a range when it comes to servings and portions. If your meal plan describes your dinner as a serving of vegetables, a protein and a starch, it's NOT the end of the world if you have an extra starch or an extra fat or an extra "whatever it may be." Don't be rigid. Be flexible. Let yourself off the hook.

In recovery, it's common for your eating disorder to try to sneak back in. It can be very confusing too. Are you thinking according to false eating disorder thoughts, or are you thinking through true thoughts of your own?

The contest here is between thoughts and feelings. It's a problem (thought influenced by your eating disorder) when it becomes a rule that you "have to eat" a food because of what it does FOR you and what it does TO you. For example, an eating disorder thought that would happen at a restaurant would influence you to order a salad because of its nutritional value and maybe its low caloric content when actually you'd rather enjoy something else on the menu. Passing up an enjoyable entrée because you "should" eat a salad is a F.E.A.R.–based thought, powered by that damn eating disorder.

Your true thought guides you to order what simply sounds appetizing, even tasty. Of course, it's important to choose an entrée that's within balance (if it's available). Your thoughts are free from an eating disorder on those occasions when you choose to eat according to your authentic self.

And with Wednesday's night of knowledge, I had a new set of weapons to fight my eating disorder.

I know how to eat healthy and get enough nutrition. I know what a portion should look like (one cup, for example). I know what a serving is and what it takes to eat a balanced meal. In no way do I want to restrict nutrition.

But (yes, there's a but) food has filled unknown holes for 15 years of my life. What's missing that I use food to replace? I'm aware that when my depression and anxiety are at their worst, I'm most likely to engage in disastrous binge eating.

I realized Wednesday night that the future was still very scary. As if I had a huge, nearly impossible algebra problem to figure out, I hadn't yet determined what caused me to fill the unknown emptiness with food. Still unclear was a way to maintain control and normalize the way I think about food, no matter my mood, sadness or worry.

I longed to realize a truth that would soon hit me: Food is not made to make you LOOK a certain way. Food is not supposed to make you FEEL a certain way about yourself. Food is made to provide fuel through nutrition and nourishment.

*I will look forward. I will look forward.*

# CHAPTER 20

# Day 17

## *Thursday, August 31*

The following day, I had a meeting with my dietician, Isabella, and I was enthusiastically eager to continue seeking answers to some lingering hard questions ... some from Wednesday that I wanted to expand on, and some that had been dancing around for a while that I hadn't quite figured out yet.

First, you can't be mindful of everything at one time. And this shouldn't be the expectation. When food-related anxiety starts to get the best of you, step back from the fret. You must give yourself compassion. For example, let's say you have an extra starch as part of a meal. This is not necessarily a bad thing. Instead, look at it with compassion— you ate a good amount of nutrition, and you had an extra serving of starch. So what? Did you enjoy the meal? Are you able to finish your day as usual? Are you able to eat again when it's time for your next meal? Will you be able to go on about the next day as planned?

Don't beat yourself up when you eat a bit outside of your balanced diet. Be gentle with yourself. That extra serving and that slight detour from a perfectly balanced meal shouldn't be enough to steal the kindness you have for the person you are inside—with or without an extra serving of food.

Food groups are workable, Isabella said.

When you find yourself in a situation where a meal doesn't cover a variety of food groups, it's OK to accept the options at hand.

Ask yourself: "I'm here, I need nutrition, and how can I be flexible?"

Back to the German festival I attended Saturday night: *"I'm here at this event, I need nutrition, and I have to be flexible with what's offered. I will eat an additional grain serving as it still gives me some nutrition and everyone needs nutrition."*

*"I did not get to eat vegetables or fruits at the festival, and in no way, shape or form should this mean I'm in debt with the vegetable food group. It will be a good idea to be mindful of Saturday night's dinner on Sunday, and if I can add in a vegetable somewhere, that would be great, but it won't make up for Saturday because there is no need to 'make up' for something that I shouldn't consider a loss."*

Second, speaking of mindfulness, what's the best approach to take when looking out for red flags that can lead to eating disorder behaviors?

Food is absolutely a source of emotion. When you experience a desire for a particular food, or when you are eating a delightful food, the "Yum!" associated with that experience is a feeling of pleasure, enjoyment and satisfaction. But how do you know if these emotions are associated with an eating disorder?

It comes down to what food is available at the time you wish to eat it. If, in fact, you have the desire for a particular food and it's unavailable at that time, be mindful of how you handle the situation. Keep your head in the game.

Someone with an eating disorder will become fixated on that one food and no other food will do. Because of the eating disorder's strong, often unbeatable commands, you'll stop at nothing to get that food. The intense craving creates a tunnel vision effect, wherein you can't see anything else except for that one food when it comes to meeting your expectations for hunger satisfaction.

Let's say someone tells you to not look at the pink elephant in the park. What do you immediately want to do?

I bet you'd immediately catch a glimpse of said pink elephant. I know I would! The undeniable strength of the pink elephant image pulls you in so that you absolutely must see it for yourself.

Someone who does not have an eating disorder will naturally step back from the desire and be OK with the absence of the particular food. He or she will think, "OK, I'm unable to eat that food right now, and I'm cool with eating the other foods that are available right now. No big deal. The other foods will suit just fine." And game over—there's no pursuit, unmet expectations, or lack of satisfaction just because he or she wasn't able to eat a particular food at a given time.

Regardless of what prompts you to desire a food, it's totally OK to want it, and to enjoy it, as long as you stay within reasonable balance.

For the ladies in the place, let's talk about a false sense of food craving: premenstrual syndrome (PMS). It's common, according to the EDTC, to associate food-related desires with *that* time of the month. Plus, because food can serve as a source of comfort during that time, it's typical to think food will aid in reducing crankiness because food can help you feel good. While PMS is a case-by-case scenario, and especially because month to month it's never the same, your best bet for recovery is to be mindful of the source of food desires. It's one thing for the thought of a food to sound good; it's another to believe it will make you feel better.

Third, what does the work look like when you're trying to minimize (not end—end follows black-and-white thinking) anxiety that's associated with food choices? Let's say it's time to choose a meal. Black-and-white thinking leads you to make a decision based on how perfectly balanced the meal is, or on how absolutely off-balanced it is. How does gray-area thinking come into play and allow you to choose a not-so-perfectly balanced meal and be OK with it?

It's important to watch out for the floodgates. In other words, just because you allow one or two extra starches, desserts, extra dairy, extra anything into the mix, don't allow the gates to open completely to the point where your entire diet is based on triggering foods. If too many triggering (often imbalanced) foods take over your diet, it could fall under an eating disorder behavior, or potentially lead to one. So it's OK to open the gate every now and then, and allow yourself the flexibility to do so, but it's also a good idea to maintain control over the floodgates.

When you crave a meal or particular food that throws your balanced diet off in a way that raises an uncomfortable red flag, take a step back and fact-check the circumstances in that moment.

- Have I eaten appropriately for the day?

If yes, allow yourself the extra food. It's OK to listen to your body and give it what it's asking for.

If no, get clear on the reason for wanting the particular food. Make sure it's legitimate hunger instead of an eating disorder disguised as hunger.

- Am I craving the food because I haven't gotten enough sleep? For example, maybe my body is feeling tired, and so it says it needs an extra carb because it knows high-carb foods are energy sources. It's not necessarily hunger that creates desire for the carb, but fatigue.
- Is my body deficient in something besides sleep, and what could this deficiency be signaling? For example, maybe the deficiency stems from a bad day and comes in the form of fulfillment or approval, and my body says it needs the extra food to feel accomplished and appreciated.

A bad day should not prompt a change in food consumption. What's the motivation to eat in whatever manner you might feel in that moment, once a bad day comes to a close?

It's not about the extra food craving being appropriately fitting or justified. It's about why you want it. If you're hungry, fine. If you're grumpy, not fine.

# CHAPTER 21

# Day 18
*Tuesday, September 5*

My next meeting with Carmen came at a critical time; I had just spent a couple days on a literal ledge or two.

That weekend, my family and I left early Friday for a hiking trip. The sun hadn't even risen yet when we hit northbound Interstate 71, en route to Cleveland, Ohio.

I had no idea that the trip would lead to more gray-area eating than I'd ever thought about preparing for. Even with long, multiple hikes during the day at Cuyhoga Valley National Park on the edge of breathtaking waterfalls and a nine-mile walk exploring the city of Cleveland, the food-related discomfort that came once I returned back home, and back to reality, pushed me way too close to a relapse. Red flags and a danger zone all around, I wanted to run away. I wanted to turn back the hands of time and do the trip all over again so I could make better eating choices.

But I couldn't.

I had to live in the gray area, in all of its bullshit glory. It nearly destroyed me and almost ruined everything I'd worked toward accomplishing in treatment. The choices I'd made felt like failure, and most certainly as if I'd committed multiple crimes. The familiar guilt had returned, along with my false need to isolate from friends and fun until the guilt went away, even though putting oneself in remorse-filled quarantine is no way to live.

Even though I knew that was my black-and-white thinking getting the best of me, it was too powerful to stop. I was trapped in a destructive gray area, and it felt like the threat of being in the eye of a hurricane—like everything you know and love could be instantly, surprisingly taken

by an uncontrollable, unpre-
dictable and deadly storm.

*I will look forward. I will look forward.*

You can imagine how it felt all too meant-to-be when I opened up my calendar the following Tuesday morning at work to see I had a meeting scheduled with Carmen for 4 p.m. It was the first move I'd made after the long Labor Day weekend to get adjusted back to the normal daily routine.

Impeccable timing.

I shared with Carmen my struggles, "confessions" and thought processes from the weekend.

When I recalled what all I had to eat during the holiday getaway, Carmen had *zero* reaction. To someone without an eating disorder, the food and desserts I ate over the weekend were perfectly normal

**My mom, Norma, and me braving a chilly Lake Erie for a photo op in Edgewater Park on September 3, 2017.**

and reasonable. *Also* to someone without an eating disorder, I'd done NOTHING wrong. I enjoyed my vacation and enjoyed the food I ate on vacation. And that's that. End of story.

It didn't feel like the end of story, though, and so I prodded Carmen for more help … help to make me feel less guilty. While it's not Carmen's job to make me feel better about myself, she added some helpful, objective context that allowed me to deal a bit better with the doubt I was experiencing—doubt so heavy I could no longer carry it around.

"Holly," Carmen said. "You say you want to work your way into the gray area, but you're here. You're *here now*."

I sat there with no response, no movement, no nothing. I'm not sure if I was too stunned to speak, too shocked to respond or simply frozen while Carmen's revolutionary idea sank in.

*I'm here! Right here in the area of imperfection. Right here in the area of utter, nearly unbearable discomfort. Right here in the midst of uncertainty. Right here in the unknown. Right here with no control. Right here where I can't comprehend my own thoughts or govern my own mental guidance. Right here in the cloudy confusion where not a damn thing makes sense, where everything seems like it needs to be fixed, and where things exist as-is in pure authenticity, no matter how uncomfortable and self-conscious I feel. I have arrived. I am here.*

As I told Carmen, being comfortable in the gray area means I'd be more easy-going than I am now. I told her that for as long as I can remember, I'd tried so incredibly hard to be easy-going and to go with the flow.

"But why do you have to try?" Carmen asked. "Why do you have to try so hard?"

Once again I sat there, immobile, trying to find the perfect answer to Carmen's question.

Can I not accept the as-is version of me, who's not always easy-going? Do I have to see my personality and failure to relax as something that needs to be improved or fixed? Why can I not just appreciate the fact that I can be a bit tense and headstrong at times?

The way I see it, if I'm more laidback, then others will like me more, and so I'll like myself more too.

The way I see it, being easy-going is a positive trait that I don't always have, and it's a positive trait that I want so badly.

Finding relaxation a little easier, going with the flow without the urge to control, and having more tolerance when things get gray all seem closely aligned to the personality of someone who's happy and gushing with joy. And if I want to be happier, and less threatened by an eating disorder, it made sense that I should pound the pavement in working toward those personality goals. **I'd yet to realize that it's OK to not be OK, that just because something isn't perfect doesn't mean there's a flaw to fix.**

Carmen's next recommended action was to stop and fact-check my thoughts and beliefs, which to me, as a professional journalist, seemed to be a very reliable practice as part of my therapy and recovery.

Beliefs:

1. I ate too much while on vacation.
2. I ate too many Fear Foods while on vacation.
3. I'm not ready to leave EDTC treatment.
4. I need to make more progress before discharge.
5. I need more help in preventing a relapse.
6. I'm not easy-going and I should be easy-going.
7. I shouldn't find it so difficult to relax.
8. There must be something wrong with me because I'm always anxious.
9. I need to fix parts of me so I can be happy.
10. I'm not cool enough for others and I'm not cool enough for myself.

Fact-checking these 10 beliefs proved them to be inaccurate. There is no evidence to prove any of them true. They're F.E.A.R.–based, false thoughts.

All it took was Carmen's non-reaction, her changeless expression when I thought I was "confessing" to eating "badly" while on vacation. The fact that Carmen's face stayed fixed and her body didn't move an inch as I spoke told me that I actually didn't eat too much while on vacation or eat too many Fear Foods while on vacation.

I decided that it was finally time to look through a new lens—a lens that allowed me to breathe a little easier and let myself off the hook, and allowed me to see a new reality: **I am good enough. I am far from perfect, but I don't need to be fixed.** People like me for me, and I like me for me too. Full disclosure: Believing this is easier said than done sometimes.

Can you imagine how unbelievably nice it feels to stop working on yourself and well, relax? The "I'm not good enough" mentality is one of the hardest mindsets to kick. And it's conflicting because you're trying to stop working on yourself while you're working to feel good enough, regardless of how you feel or circumstances that make you feel the need to change.

Just be. And leave it blank.

*I will look forward. I will look forward.*

Carmen recommended that as part of my continued outpatient treatment, I maintain the ability to see things in a different way. Again, with no more group treatment, I'd have to work extra hard on my own.

An idiosyncrasy is a behavior or a way of thought that's particular to an individual. Being highly adaptable and willing to see the other side of the coin is important for progress made in outpatient therapy, as you'll be challenged to change your mind.

Looking ahead with individual therapy on the horizon, **I knew that adaptability, flexibility, patience and a bright attitude would be crucial in my success with therapy and eating disorder recovery.** So I invited them along for the ride.

～

Lo and behold, I arrived home from therapy with just enough time to have a plumber service my broken toilet while I put away clean laundry before my first-ever fantasy football draft. And September 5 marked #NationalCheesePizzaDay on social media. And that's all I needed for an excellent reason to eat cheese pizza!

I ordered a medium cheese pizza, without extra cheese because I didn't want this pizza to be perfect. I wanted it to be a gray-area pizza. I ordered it from an average local delivery chain because I didn't want the restaurant choice to be perfect either. I added three chocolate chip cookies to the order, just because they sounded very tasty.

The pizza arrived to my door and smelled delightful, just the way a fresh cheese pizza should smell! I finished the whole pizza pie, minus the crust, and stopped after the second cookie.

I'm unsure if it was a binge or not. I felt hungry after each slice and the hunger continued through the whole pie. Maybe it was a baby step toward the realization that there's no such thing as a cheat meal, a good or bad meal, and that the pizza and cookies were, simply put, just dinner. It was also a baby step toward a new belief that the Fear Food meal doesn't have to be finished in one sitting. Even if it was just one tiny step, it was a step in the right direction: acceptance.

# CHAPTER 22

# Day 19

## *Wednesday, September 6,*
## *the Last Night*

I didn't want to attend treatment Wednesday, but it wasn't due to resentment or dread of the three hours that were ahead of me. It was because I wasn't ready to say goodbye.

I'd been thinking about my final check-in sheet for days. How would my mood, irritability and anxiety rank? What current thoughts, feelings and experiences would I have to report? Would I have to record binge eating or restricting? And, of course, what support would I need?

The last night at the EDTC felt anything but celebratory, and I felt nowhere near the finish line. The treatment room felt especially somber, yet bittersweet Wednesday evening.

On the check-in sheet, I scored my anxiety as a 9, my irritability a 5 and my mood a 6, all on a scale of 1 to 10. Of course my anxiety almost hit the top mark.

At that moment, I doubted the EDTC's program more than ever. The fact that on my last night, my anxiety was the highest it had been over the span of treatment disproved the program's effectiveness altogether. If the treatment had worked, my anxiety should have significantly decreased, right?

I would soon see my anxiety in a new light.

All I knew Wednesday was that I wasn't ready to step away from a treatment program that had unexpectedly become such a big part of my life. After all, I spent the same amount of time at the EDTC per week as I'd spend at a part-time job. Not only did it take up every Monday and Wednesday evening and Saturday morning, it had become a priority.

It had become something that actually helped keep my general anxiety in check because I knew there was somewhere I needed to be. I no longer had to figure out how to spend every Monday and Wednesday evening or Saturday morning. The figuring out was done for me. Even though I didn't always look forward to being at the EDTC and would rather be at 100 other places, I didn't have to think about where and how to spend that time and so my mind felt a much-needed sense of stillness.

Free time has been a forever struggle of mine. I cannot be OK, and just chill, without the need to serve a purpose for some given chunk of the day. I can't watch hours of Netflix like others can because I feel like I should be more productive with that time, even though getting lost in good ol' TV shows sounds wonderful. The only way I'm able to stop and spend hours on the couch is if the to-do list is absolutely complete and I have no obligation left to meet (which is rare if not nonexistent).

Errand to run? Run it. Something is dirty? Get up and clean it. Friend I need to call? Pick up the phone. A yoga class starting soon? Go take it. A topic I'd like to be more knowledgeable about? Research it. Do it. Do it all. I won't rest. Not until it's all done to the best of my ability.

*What can I do today? What SHOULD I do today? What will make me feel whole? What will make me feel accomplished? What will quiet and lower my anxiety? What will bring me joy? Peace? Love? What if I get sad because I'm alone? What if I get bored? What if I arrive at near anxiety-induced panic?*

*And what if I turn to food?*

The "have to be there" element that the EDTC added to my life was a very good thing—it kept me from pressure I feel whenever I'm on my own.

On that particular Wednesday, I felt like I was too far away from establishing the desired comfort or acceptance that I expected to come with a new way of thinking and eating: life in the gray area.

I was experiencing the gray area that evening, but it was too gray just yet. It was uncomfortably gray. It was eerie, icky and painted in shades of panic.

I told my peers and EDTC staff that I'd spent days thinking about how I'd show up to and spend my final night. Nonetheless, I threw my thoughts out there and let my guard down. I knew that if any time was the most crucial for me to present my authentic self and practice vulnerability, Wednesday night was that chance. There would be no do-overs.

"I feel too gray," I told the group, "to the point I'm cautioned that I'm in a danger zone with guilt and eating disorder habits."

As if Emma, one of the EDTC's dieticians, knew what I was thinking, she hit the nail on the head with her feedback-filled response.

She said my exceptionally high anxiety made total sense because that meant my treatment and my practice were working. Through *practice*, I'd been addressing the worry that comes with imperfection. I'd been experiencing the unfamiliar gray area more than I'd ever allowed myself to before. The more distress I expose myself to, the more anxiety I'll feel. And the more practicing imperfection I do, the more comfortable I'll become with gray thinking rather than black and white.

So the jump in anxiety, although it felt terrible, was to be expected. Like it was supposed to happen, like it was part of the grand design.

So there I was, right there in the thick of the work, and I was getting my ass handed to me, too.

I was discounting my experiences and emotions because they made me feel defeated. They made me feel like I'd never get where I want to be and maybe I should just give up and accept that **freedom of imperfection** was just too far out of reach.

Instead, I should do the opposite: immerse myself in the anxiety and allow myself to feel the pain, fret and sadness it brought. It would be that practice and training that would make the difference.

Let's say you're assigned homework from your algebra teacher. You bring the assignment home, sit down to complete the work, and you find that the problems are impossible to solve. You come up with wrong answers time and time again, and you just cannot determine what "x" equals. You have to do more than *wish* to figure out the equation. You have to work for it.

You must at least make an attempt to solve the equation. You likely have to make multiple attempts. Perhaps you need to stay after class for extra help or even seek support from a tutor. You must not give up. You have to do the work.

Anxiety and an eating disorder work the same way. You have an assignment—to cope with anxiety and an eating disorder—and you *wish* to have the ability to do so. Well, you might sit down with that assignment and find that it can't be accomplished with one try. You have to work the problems over and over, perhaps with help from others. You have to discover what works and what doesn't work. Never give up. Keep pressing through the work.

The more practice you get solving algebra problems, the better you'll get at finding the answers.

And trust me, I bet you're far better at math than I'll ever be!

The more you practice coping with anxiety and an eating disorder, the better you'll get at managing them.

You have to be exposed to the algebra, and you have to be exposed to anxiety and an eating disorder. **Only through exposure can transformation eventually take place.**

When Wednesday night's exercise began, thankfully there was no arithmetic to work out! Instead, we designed an experiment that would test our predictions about a dietary "rule"—a rule that only an eating disorder's F.E.A.R.–based thinking could create.

Heaviness hung over the group with massive weight sitting on our shoulders. I could tell this would be a very tough exercise. Before we even got started, we reacted to the very thought of putting the experiment to the test.

*I'm going to find evidence that could help squash my bullshit story.*

*The experiment could generate a very positive outcome and realization.*

*The experiment is scary, and it's a way to uncover a reality that I'm unable to see at this time.*

The experiment was broken down into five steps, which started with describing a dietary rule I try to follow in order to prevent binge eating.

*I must eat 100 percent according to my balanced, planned meals so that I stay in a good spot with the lowest possible risk of binge eating.*

Second, if my eating disorder could talk, what would it say would happen if I break my dietary rule?

*If I venture too far away from balanced, planned meals, then I will binge eat.*

How will I know if my eating disorder's prediction comes true?

*There's only one way to find out. Eat gray, observe how I feel, and see what happens.*

As the third step, how can I design an experiment to test the accuracy of my eating disorder's prediction?

*Plan out a week's worth of meals, and strategically incorporate a firm number of Fear Foods.*

Fourth, what other predictions are possible? Since my eating disorder is great at catastrophizing, it might have additional predictions in store.

*I'll ruin all progress I've made toward reaching my highest level of confidence, best state of health and greatest ability to refrain from a relapse. Plus, I'll always have to engage in restricting if I eat "this" and "that."*

Are there any possible positive outcomes?

*I uncover and adopt new comforts and habits, from which Fear Foods become normal and there are no longer thoughts that associate Fear Foods with apprehension and threat.*

*I'll break the association between Fear Foods and skin problems, weight gain and increased irritability.*

*I'll see a significant improvement in social anxiety and less desire to isolate myself from others.*

*There are no good or bad foods. There's no moral compass pointing toward what's right and wrong in eating habits and food choices.*

For the fifth and last step, complete the experiment. What actually happens?

*I'll start tomorrow. This is my last night in Intensive Outpatient treatment. I have no other choice.*

The exercise was hands down the best way to see what living and eating would look like after transitioning away from the EDTC's care. The fearful "what if" questions would be tested during the experiment, and I'd find out how change and how new ways of thinking would feel. I'd test the borders between Fear Foods and binge eating, hopefully reaching some goals along the way.

*Lose the idea that "'Such and such' food is good" and "'Such and such' food is bad."*

*Break the connection between emotion and food. Emotions and foods are two very different, unrelated parts of life.*

*Detach from believing that one eating disorder engagement negates any and all progress made during recovery.*

The experiment, along with other exercises and guidance provided at the EDTC, is all about finding new neural pathways—the series of connected nerves along which electrical impulses travel through the body, and also the route information takes to reach your brain and then travel from one region of the brain to another.

The good news? You're not stuck with the neural pathways you were born with. Those roads can be demolished and then rebuilt. The more you challenge new neural pathways (finding new routes), the more routine they become.

I'm no rocket scientist, but think about it: How often do you look back at the end of your day and recall specific details about your commute to work that morning? If you're like me, you drove through your neighborhood, hopped on the highway, exited the highway once you got downtown and then parked in a parking garage, all while music is blaring and you're belting out every lyric to every song.

And generally speaking, the drive to work follows the same routine, and so there's nothing that especially stands out to remember or reflect on.

Your eating habits work the same way—there are so many possible routes to take from meal to meal. In the early stages of managing an eating disorder, there's a lot to think about, many decisions to make and endless trials to take on.

But as you challenge and repeat processes of recovery, new eating habits will become more regular. You'll repeat the habits more and more until you find what works best for you, putting little thought into getting them right.

For example, as I incorporate Fear Food into my regular diet instead of seeing Fear Food as a destructive cheat meal, that Fear Food will become more routine, and so will my thinking habits that pertain to them.

There's one more step to take. I'll bet that at least once, if not a handful of times, you've run into a traffic jam, construction, a vehicle accident, and detours on your routine drive to work.

So then your route changes. Either you have to wait until the cars move again, you have to maneuver your vehicle around road work, you have to wait until the wreck clears so it takes longer to get to work, or you have to detour and take a different course.

As you develop new neural pathways in your eating disorder

recovery, chances are you'll also run into some traffic jams, construction, accidents and detours. And by putting in work, you'll finally start moving again, you'll find your way around the construction, you'll make it beyond the accident, and you'll find your way again after driving off course for a bit.

**No matter what, your final destination is clear: eating disorder recovery.**

My "last meal" at the EDTC was … well … routine. The all-too-familiar roasted pork, garlic mashed potatoes and cooked veggies for everyone else, raw carrots for me.

I could have eaten more than the portion I was allowed, and I knew that it would get the job done for dinner, and that I could grab a snack at home later if I needed. Above any concern over dinner and emotion that dinner stirred, I wanted my last dinner at the EDTC to go smoothly, without conflict and without being served a Boost.

And so it did.

I was geared up for Process Group after dinner. I couldn't wait to talk about self-doubt, because if there was one powerful lesson I would leave with Wednesday night, I believed that new insights about self-doubt would put me on the trajectory to finish strong and walk away feeling complete and with a new sense of self-esteem.

Indeed, Process went terribly and I wasn't ready for the group's reaction coming at me. The room's unease became suffocating, and the more I spoke, the more misunderstood I felt.

Process was gray. I mean, GRAY.

I shared my tendency to pick up on likable characteristics of other people because I felt like if I acted in those ways, I'd be more liked by others. For example, Harper is very likable. She's a theater major in college and I like the dramatic way she expresses herself and the alliterative way she proudly speaks. If I adopt those behaviors from Harper, maybe I'll be a better person.

Generally speaking, I'd assumed a fixed mindset that everyone else is happy with themselves, including the goods and not so goods. That because everyone else was content and comfortable in their own skin, they loved themselves for who they are without feeling a need to change. Meanwhile, I couldn't silence the nonstop question running through my mind: What do I have to do so that I can simply be happy too?

Next, there's Phoebe. Her humor, big personality and just-the-right amount of sarcasm are irresistible. She must have more friends than she can count. While I have a sense of humor drier than the Sahara, Phoebe's spin on humor must keep everyone laughing. Maybe if I were funnier, like Phoebe, people would like me more.

As I was sharing these thoughts with my peers, I couldn't believe what Phoebe said as she interrupted me.

"Why are you telling us these things, Holly? Are you fishing for compliments?" she asked.

No! No no no no no! Not my intention in the slightest bit!

What I wanted was insight that would allow me to understand why I try to be like others sometimes and why I can't be happy with myself. I was desperately seeking advice on how to up my self-confidence game, not compliments. I thought that with the feedback of others, I could strengthen the way I see myself without trying to mimic the amusing, desirable habits I see in others.

Incredibly offended by Phoebe's question, I felt myself back away from anything she had to say going forward. I wanted to run from the insulting comment, and I didn't want it to hurt me. I wanted to un-like Phoebe despite how much she'd helped me during Intensive Outpatient treatment.

And so I sat there, forcing myself to give her the benefit of the doubt. Maybe she genuinely misunderstood me. Maybe she doesn't think I'm a self-absorbed, pathetic asshole like her question made me feel. Maybe I should look beyond her comment and just keep going. Keep listening. Keep being there. Keep learning. Keep practicing gray-area thinking and living.

People with an eating disorder, as I learned from my EDTC peers, spend way too much time telling themselves they're not good enough, and that's exactly what I'd done for 15 years. I couldn't see myself as satisfactory, so I assumed how others saw me and I allowed that assumption to be influenced by my own low self-esteem and insecurities. And guilt. And shame.

If I can't give myself a clean slate, that doesn't mean others won't. If I can't see myself without blemishes and flaws, that doesn't mean others can't like me anyway. It doesn't mean they can see those imperfections and faults. Just because I've made a lot of mistakes, that doesn't mean others are going to hold them against me or walk away because of them.

I had become blind to how likable I really am. **Likability and close relationships based on unconditional love had become something I could only wish for.**

If there's a mistake to call out it's this: **Taking on the behaviors and personality traits of others makes you inauthentic.** Why would you not want to be real? If you're acting in a way that doesn't represent your authentic self, you're probably not acting according to your values. Instead, live according to what's most important to you, and love the time you spend doing so!

For example, let's say you value honesty. If you're not a very funny person and suddenly you begin cracking jokes all the time, you're not demonstrating your values in life and you're not expressing what's important to you.

I value authenticity. Although I've been off track before, I want people to like me because I'm real. If I say I will do something, I'll do it. If I tell you I'm feeling a certain way, then I really do feel that way. If I get involved in a cause that's important to me, it means that cause really does hit home. If I spend my time doing something I enjoy, then that activity really does add joy to my life. And when I say I'm telling the truth, I'm being as (sometimes brutally) honest as it gets.

There will never be a time when I'm OK with being fake in my relationships with others. So when I've assumed habits, mannerisms and qualities of others, I've in fact acted in a way that's out of alignment with my true self—who I really am at my core, in my heart and in my soul.

Be sure to remember this: It's very hard to be authentic every day. You might not be your true self every day. The reason your behavior and attitude can teeter is because you're not in the same environment and circumstance every day. Each day ebbs and flows, and that's OK.

Maybe you're comfortable being funny around some people and in some scenarios, but in others you feel better being more serious. For example, you might act in a way at work that ensures your credibility and that promotes your responsibility and capability to highly perform at your job. Perhaps there's little time for laughter.

And then outside of your work, you're with your friends and family who dig your humor. You might act in a way that requires less credibility, accountability and professionalism—you might loosen up, joke around, relax and have more room for amusement.

The same goes for a first date, meeting a new group of peers, etc. You have your authentic self in all situations, and it doesn't have to be the same across the board. You're able to have a true self in one scenario and a true self in another. There's a place and time for everything. That's just reality.

It's not your responsibility to fully show up every day, and in fact, that's an unreal expectation.

Let's take a look at an important truth: **When you show people who you really are, they won't want to push you away.** Through their eyes, you're good enough. You're exceptional. You're extraordinary.

In a relationship that's authentic and truly genuine, you won't be liked for what you own, what you've won and what you've achieved. You'll be liked for the love and joy you can offer, how you make others feel, and who you are at your core.

You might be kind, and you might be generous, and you might be funny, and you might be a blast to be around. But you don't have to possess every good quality to be good enough, exceptional or extraordinary. One or two qualities are just enough to be *perfectly* YOU.

Toward the end of Wednesday's treatment, Phoebe asked if there was anything special I'd like to do.

I did have a little something up my sleeve.

As I told the group, loneliness is one of the quickest ways to ignite my eating disorder. Loneliness is the prime reason I'd binge eat. Loneliness had a way of making me feel so insufferably sad. It's something I'd never want anyone else to endure.

And so I wanted to provide a way to prevent others from going through loneliness as it can be the toughest, most painful feeling to handle. I told my peers that I'd like for them all to have a way to reach me if they felt lonely, and also have someone there who understands their struggles, as I'd been through it firsthand. I was still going through the eating disorder motions. We all were going through eating disorder therapy and prevention. Together.

I passed around my business card. That way, my peers had the phone number of someone who, no matter what might be needed, would do whatever it took to help.

I wasn't sure if anyone would reach out or not, but at least they knew they could and they had the means to reach me.

Phoebe also asked if there was a ceremony I'd like to hold—walking through a "peer tunnel," striking a gong, or any of a few other festive ways to leave the EDTC in triumph for my final exit.

I declined the ceremony and preferred we all leave as we normally would—"the usual." I didn't feel my exit was anything worth celebrating. I hadn't crossed the finish line. Instead, I was only starting a new race on a new track.

The second I walked through the door of my condo Wednesday night, I felt utter disappointment that brought me to tears until I crawled into bed.

The last EDTC hurrah ended very awkwardly, with very little acknowledgment from my peers. In no way did I want to be showered with praise and the feeling that I'd be missed, and I didn't want to leave just like it was any other night either.

Everyone who attended Intensive Outpatient treatment that Wednesday, thanks to my business card, now knew my last name, employer, email address and phone number. But I had a weird feeling that no one would call.

*Do I really doubt myself that much?* What's up with this "No one cares to know me or like me" F.E.A.R.–based thought that I just can't kick?

Besides my external experience with everyone, including my favorite therapist Phoebe, I was overwhelmingly saddened by the separation that now existed between the EDTC and myself.

I felt like something had been taken away from me, like I'd been stripped of a sense of belonging—all valuable parts of my life that I didn't realize meant so much during treatment. I was on my own, and I didn't like that feeling, not one bit. I felt empty, like I'd encountered a downright sickening loss.

*I just don't feel any different. I just don't.*

Before I knew it, my face fell into my hands and I sobbed.

*I don't want to continue the commitment of treatment. It's so much pressure. I'll enjoy regaining the three-times-weekly windows of time. But it's scary without them. What if my anxiety spikes? What if I have nowhere to turn? I feel like I could relapse. I've overeaten daily since Friday and what if I can't stop? My body has lost muscle tone since Friday since I allowed the overeating to happen. But stop, Holly! You can't think like that. That's wrong ... no ... not wrong ... that's ineffective. The EDTC uses "ineffective" instead of "wrong" to avoid judgment. Your thinking is ineffective, Holly. Ineffective.*

*AND, you have to be strong. You HAVE to be stronger than this eating disorder. This is YOUR recovery. And you're in control.* **You deserve control, you deserve recovery and you deserve freedom and contentment.**

I wasn't sure when I'd stop crying that night, even if it meant sometime in my sleep. I felt too many thoughts at one time, keeping me from getting a grip on reality. My mind was exhausted; literally, I just couldn't take any more thought processing. My body trembled from uncertainty, tears streamed down my cheeks from sadness, and my soul was paralyzed by confusion. So on Wednesday night, I went to sleep—right smack dab in the middle of the gray area—as uncomfortable and as scary as it could ever get.

**I will look forward. I will look forward.**

# CHAPTER 23

# One Week After Discharge
## Wednesday, September 13

One week ago, I stepped away from the EDTC and into a world that would require me to manage my eating disorder alone.

I fight back tears and my eyes burn as I write this evening. I miss spending time at the EDTC with peers who share my struggle. I feel the support that once held my hand has decided to let me go. I miss being in a safe place three times per week, where I'm allowed to openly share my thoughts, experiences and shameful ways of being.

It was only at the EDTC that I could speak explicitly about my down times without being judged. I could share the darkest despair and disturbing emotions, and I could feel comfort because someone else understood, because they'd been there, or somewhere very similar, firsthand.

At the EDTC, I never had to worry about anyone turning his or her back on me. Maybe my peers and I didn't see eye to eye each session, but the genuine support remained constant no matter what. Even though I hadn't established a close friendship with my EDTC peers, they'd prove a F.E.A.R.-based thought of mine to be wrong: I'm not cool enough for others and I'm not cool enough for myself.

I never knew exactly what would take place outside the EDTC walls, but during each three-hour block I spent there, I was able to be me—the "Type-A me" that comes with an eating disorder, anxiety and obsessive behaviors, strong opinions and too many flaws to count.

When I wasn't at the EDTC, I'd almost reached a point where I'd keep all food-associated feelings to myself instead of telling others about what I was experiencing with food in that moment. It was as if sharing my contemplations would be useless.

"Oh, so you're trying to be more healthy," my family would say.

"But you're so fit, look at those muscles," my friends would say.

"Aw, that's so sad," another friend would say about my mental illness.

"I can't finish my meal, would you like the rest?"

"Are you sure you're OK to go out for dinner?"

"Don't worry, calories don't count today."

"It's cool. Just eat your feelings!"

My family and friends just don't get it like my peers and therapists at the EDTC do. Comments and reactions, and most of all, judgments, from people on the outside could send me over the edge at the drop of a hat—straight for the black area, straight for failure and rejection of all possible solutions. I didn't want to patiently explain how their comments so negatively impacted me, or why it was so important for me to avoid eating disorder-triggering talk. I wanted my family and friends to automatically, effortlessly understand as thoroughly as my EDTC support system did. It was an unrealistic expectation, but I felt too exhausted to put in any work.

My 35th birthday arrives in just over two weeks. I'm excited to go for a celebratory dinner with my family and closest friends. And I'm also dreading it, because this means my anxiety will demand a seat at the dinner table.

I'm sure everyone, excluding my anxiety, will have a blast, but I bet that while I enjoy my dinner, a celebration and great company, no one will quite understand where my head is and why.

SO HELP ME, if someone, on my birthday at the dinner table says, "Don't worry, calories don't count today."

***I will look forward. I will look forward.***

As much as I miss regular Intensive Outpatient treatment sessions at the EDTC, I'm mad at the EDTC too.

The misunderstanding that took place when Phoebe questioned if I wanted to receive compliments during my last Process hasn't been fixed. My failure to complete the discharge survey hasn't been fixed. The awkward departure that went down last week hasn't been fixed. The drop in communication since last week and my lack of effort to reach out hasn't been fixed.

Thinking about the imperfect aspects of my final night at the EDTC and the unresolved feelings I have about the defective facets puts me right back at square one: trying to make something perfect. Trying to escape black-and-white thinking.

Maybe, just maybe, the gray conditions that exist between the EDTC and me are actually normal. Maybe there are no defects at all and those beliefs were all created within me, by my overanalyzing habits and lack of patience.

Or maybe I'm avoiding follow-up contact with the EDTC because reaching out would open doors for gray-area emotions. After all, I'd have to face Phoebe, the survey, and the feeling that the EDTC staff just sent me on my way and stopped caring about me.

As of this night, one week post-discharge, I'm unclear on what action to take, what to think or what tomorrow holds.

Do I sit in the gray area and force myself to feel its discomfort? Do I call the EDTC tomorrow and tie up loose ends? Or if I make the call, will it be a bad idea because it will mean I'm trying to repair feelings that are actually gray and OK?

For now, it's all just going to be gray and I'm just going to be undecided. And that's not a bad thing. The loose ends feel messy, as if they need to be mended, and I have to allow myself to feel them as they are: frayed and GRAY.

The free time added to my schedule when EDTC treatments ended allowed me to return to my regular yoga routine. More time on my mat would be a very good thing, as yoga allows me to put my wandering mind at rest, or at least at *somewhat* of a pause. As many yogis say, the practice is an outlet to feeling light and free rather than burdened by life's heavy pressure and expectations, even if that means hitting the grocery store or getting laundry done. It's a shared belief in the yoga world that the more yoga you do, the less stress you feel, and so the more kind you are. And I believe every bit of it!

I took a class taught by someone I hadn't seen in quite some time, and it came with an unexpected, much-needed bonus: the transition back to yoga allowed for the perfect opportunity to address a friend who'd let me down and to reconnect with her because even though we hadn't spoken in a while my caring about her never faded.

Tonya and I have been friends for nearly four years, as I met her at a yoga studio when I first moved to Cincinnati in 2013.

When I think of Tonya, I picture the ultimate yogi that so many aspiring yogis wish to be—Tonya never takes life too seriously, spends a considerable amount of time in a wonderful, bliss-filled "la-la land," has the best intentions under the sun, and loves others with all her heart.

Tonya does not share the Type A, rigid, driven personality of mine. And I don't think she fully gets the anxiety and heaviness I often deal with. Tonya's free-spirited poise is a gift of hers, and especially as a yoga teacher, she shares those great vibes with everyone she has in class as well as everyone she passes while walking down the street.

Our difference in personalities has led to a couple temporary breaks in our friendship. I took a step back because I was convinced that I couldn't rely on Tonya. At times, jealousy got in the way because I had to work so much harder than Tonya to feel happiness. Tonya is so free— emotionally, financially and even schedule wise. Often, I felt like Tonya couldn't understand the serious side of life and she couldn't relate to the responsibilities and pressure I had on my plate.

I held onto an overwhelming amount of envy because I felt so many burdens and Tonya felt so much bliss.

As Merriam-Webster defines it, "la-la land" is "a euphoric dream-like mental state detached from the harsher realities of life." And I wanted to be in that world instead of a world I believed was nothing but stress and oftentimes, sadness. And it was my own fault that I couldn't experience la-la land because I couldn't accept that so much of my stress came from within.

As a disastrous way of protecting myself, I tunneled away from Tonya.

And she did nothing wrong.

There were a handful of times when Tonya had talked about getting together to kayak, to hike, to introduce me to her guy friend who was single, to attend events, etc., but she never followed through. Our friendship pretty much remained within the walls of the yoga studio, and I found myself wanting a friendship with Tonya in which we actually did the things we talked about doing.

I'd stamped an "unreliable" label on Tonya and on her potential to be a good friend. And because she had one flaw that I perceived to be potentially hurtful, I stepped away so that I couldn't possibly be exposed to pain.

One evening during the week after EDTC treatment, courage took full control of my hands and my voice, and I found myself looking up Tonya's contact information on my phone, hitting "call," and greeting her when she answered the phone.

We hadn't spoken in months.

I explained to Tonya that her tendency to not follow through with plans seemed like "all talk" and that I'd expected action. I let Tonya know it hurt my feelings because it cut deep, all the way to my childhood when my parents did quite a bit of talking but never brought ideas to fruition. I remember wondering if I was the only kid who had never visited Walt Disney World. I wondered if I wasn't good enough to go to Walt Disney World. If it were too magical of a place for "little, average me."

I told Tonya about my eating disorder and Intensive Outpatient treatment, and that it had, in fact, taken up a lot of time. I described some lessons I'd learned and said I had a lot of hope amidst a lot of fear and confusion.

I invited Tonya back into my life, asking for someone I could trust. As I told Tonya, I have a good heart and plenty of love to offer, but I'm fragile right now and can only feel comfortable giving that love to a trustworthy source. I was at a point where I needed authentic love more than I needed air and water.

Of course, the conversation ended wonderfully, and I took Tonya's yoga class that Saturday morning. With good "juju" in the air, we picked up right where we left off: on our yoga mats, flowing, giggling and sending out buckets of love.

The tough conversation with Tonya couldn't have been a better way for me to creep into the gray area and prove to myself that I'd be OK. Plus, I learned the lesson that while I was very in tune with my feelings about the situation, I should have been more empathetic in the way I related to Tonya. With an open heart, I've come to love Tonya without any expectation.

And with an open heart, anything becomes possible! I may have broken ground on learning to free myself from the need to be perfect, but my friendship with Tonya provided a platform to truly accept others and their flaws and to love them unconditionally. It's not about all being well in MY world, which my anxiety led me to believe, but it's about all being well in everyone's worlds, no matter how gray things may seem from the outside looking in.

When you're able to accept the gray areas of life, you're able to strip unnecessary judgment from people and circumstances that actually shouldn't be judged at all. It's about healing from mental illness, and along that journey, learning the unnecessary role that judgment tends to play.

Big takeaway here: Judgment only lights the fire for black-and-white thinking. Instead, when something seems gray, give that F.E.A.R.–based thought a judgment-free, gentle touch. Doing so brings freedom and unconditional love to the table, which feels unbelievably good to EVERYONE sitting around it.

Immersing myself back into yoga that Saturday reminded me of awareness and its importance as we move from day to day, moment to moment.

Just because we're aware of something doesn't mean it has to be pretty. It doesn't mean we have to make it pretty either.

Those 75 minutes of yoga proved another F.E.A.R.–based thought to be false: I need to fix parts of me so I can be happy.

Awareness of something in its existing condition allows you to accept it as-is. If you're cool with it in its current state, there's no need to change, improve or "fix" anything.

If we're talking yoga, for example, maybe you can't touch your toes. Maybe you can't stand on your head. Maybe you can't balance on one foot.

Become aware of your body's limitations. And accept them. Embrace them.

And as yoga is a practice, it's totally expected to work on building strength and flexibility. Refining the alignment of each pose is also part of yoga, but you should realize and understand that if someone else can touch their toes, stand on their head and balance on one foot, it doesn't mean he or she is a better person than people who can't.

Be aware of what you can do and cannot do, and don't try to change those conditions. Live with your body's abilities and love your body for what you can do while finding peace in what you cannot do.

As for an eating disorder, maybe you're not always able to control your eating behaviors, and maybe you can't freely rummage through your pantry without anxiety tugging at your mind. Maybe you can't stroll though a grocery store without carrying fear around in the shopping cart.

Become aware of your eating disorder's triggers, susceptibility and the impact it has on your day.

Through exposure therapy, mindfulness and other tools provided by the EDTC, use awareness of your condition and practice gaining strength and flexibility when you're faced with eating disorder challenges. Practice control over food, practice the freedom of selecting a meal from your pantry, and practice courage when shopping for groceries.

Someone without an eating disorder is not a better person than you are. He or she just doesn't have the condition. An eating disorder does not define you, nor does it affect your ability to love others and be kind, generous and true. Become aware of the powerful, gracious person you are, regardless of your eating disorder. Through awareness, **you can (and will) find ease in living with an eating disorder**.

# CHAPTER 24

# Two and a Half Weeks
# Post Treatment

*Sunday, September 23*

Eating disorder management calls for plenty of self-care, and without a doubt, self-care should feel good. Blissfully, effortlessly good.

The self-care experts at the Brooklyn-based online wellness publication www.mindbodygreen.com say taking care of yourself is just as important as taking care of others. It's all about being kind, compassionate and loving—and don't those always feel good?

A regular, dedicated practice of self-care helps remove the self-hate that so many of us likely feel occasionally, some more often than others. An eating disorder is closely linked to feelings of self-hate. It encourages thoughts of worthlessness and emptiness, disgust and inadequacy. Self-hate triggers eating disorder behaviors because when your eating disorder attacks, it's a fight that can seem impossible to win.

When I would binge eat, I'd feel meaningless, like I was a disgrace that didn't deserve to see another day. It would make me feel like I had nothing good on the inside to offer, like I was incapable of adding value to someone's life, including my own. It made me feel dreadful and ugly—too ugly to go outside and in no way be seen in the public eye. After an episode of binge eating, I believed that I'd never be good enough, qualified enough, or eligible enough for anything, and at times, that included getting help. **At the scariest times, that meant I wasn't eligible for life.**

There were mornings after a night's binge when I'd drive to work and imagine myself getting into a fatal traffic accident on I-71 because I felt like I deserved for my life to end.

Self-care is so important because it can lead to a free, beautiful lifestyle. And if you're doing self-care right, it should naturally feel good. It should be effortless; please never feel like you have to TRY to feel worth, beauty and abundance. It is already inside of you, ready to nurture your soul and deliver joy to your heart. Trust that you need to add nothing more to yourself. Trust that you are cherished, lovely, and perfectly imperfect as you are, in this very moment. Right here, right now. Today.

Self-care is much more than rest, yoga and fitness, meditation and bubble baths.

It's deeper than that.

Take a few minutes to think about the desires your mind, body and soul long for the most. Perhaps it's travel, a chance to share your creative skills or an opportunity to overcome fear. Guess what? Book your flight, start your blog and go bungee jumping. **Ignite self-care by bringing your BIG dreams to life.**

Snap out of your routine to give yourself a little TLC. Change the way you get ready for work in the morning, try taking different routes when on the go, mix in a phone call to a friend during your evening of rest and relaxation, try a new yoga class, get a massage, take a day trip … the sky's the limit here. No matter what the alteration to your routine might be, do it and note how you feel. The slightest bit of novelty can do wonders for your mind's refresh button. Let your soul guide you and give shift a go.

Perhaps the most important element in self-care is celebration of small victories.

And so I threw a party about two weeks after treatment.

I was at the grocery store on a very quick run for deodorant, toilet paper and laundry detergent.

I'd already decided that pasta sounded good for dinner. Believe it or not, plain spaghetti noodles sprinkled generously with Parmesan cheese makes for one of my favorite meals. Simple and maybe even bland, I enjoy it. Taste, texture and all.

A big spaghetti dinner would have counted as a cheat meal before getting help for my eating disorder, because a reasonable portion of pasta was never a consideration. The spaghetti meal would have turned into a F.E.A.R.–based, binge-eating blowout with its heap of melted mozzarella cheese, nearly a jar of Parmesan, olive oil, all a specific brand

I turned to when I "needed" to go all out with a cheat meal. And because each bite had to be the perfect bite, and because the feast had to be my very last regretful, guilt-filled cheat meal, I'd make multiple trips to the microwave to make sure every nook and cranny of the pasta was sizzling hot until my plate was cleared. Anxiety would pack my condo from wall to wall, and when I finished the spaghetti-turned-binge-eat-feast, it would be followed up with a F.E.A.R.–based, ginormous dessert, eaten in the same binge-eating manner as so many times before, panic going berserk inside of me.

On that errand, the thought of buying F.E.A.R.–based ingredients for my spaghetti dinner was hardly there. Thoughts whispered to me a couple times while in the store, but truthfully, I never even made it over to the dairy section, where the special cheese was stocked. I remembered my pantry and fridge at home, and the fact that some (a.k.a. ENOUGH) spaghetti noodles and Parmesan cheese were already there, and so there was no need to buy any extras.

It hit me later that evening while home folding laundry with Sunday's NFL games on television…

*I didn't need to buy binge-eating food! I didn't even really think very much about it! I didn't feel very anxious while in the grocery store. The temptation was there, but it wasn't strong enough to push me into binge-eating action. This is awesome. What a great feeling! What a great show of progress! Way to go!*

A tiny celebration to add to the spaghetti success: For one of the first times I can remember, I had leftovers to toss in a glass dish and store in the fridge. I'd never left food to keep and eat at a later time. I'd gorge on the entire pot, no matter how much spaghetti I prepared.

When I started cooking that evening, I wrapped my hands around the durum flour-based dry pasta, broke it into three sections, and then dropped it in a large pot to boil. From there, the al dente pasta went into a colander and it was time to eat. Using a slotted spoon, I put three scoops into a medium bowl and carried on with a dusting of Parmesan cheese.

I looked from the colander, which held plenty of yummy pasta, to my dish, which also held plenty of yummy pasta.

I looked back at the colander. I looked back at my dish.

I looked back at the colander. I looked back at my dish.

I held my gaze on my dish, cradling a healthy portion of spaghetti, and I took several deep breaths. My breathing was audible and I controlled the length of the inhales and exhales until the slightest calm crept into my being.

Then I picked up my dish and carried it to my dinner table to enjoy.

I had very little desire to eat more spaghetti when I finished my meal. I knew that if I went in for seconds, it would take me over the edge and I'd be in binge-eating territory. And I knew—no matter what—I couldn't let that happen.

Once I was back in my kitchen and my dirty dish was in the sink, I picked up the slotted spoon and emptied the colander, put the pasta in a glass Pyrex container and in the fridge … where leftovers belong.

No matter how small the win might seem, it deserves every bit of celebration. Be sure to throw each tiny victory the biggest bash of triumph.

The small accomplishment was just enough to negate a couple more of my F.E.A.R.–based thoughts and allowed me to see that, in fact, I didn't need to make more progress before EDTC discharge or need more help from the EDTC to prevent a relapse. I'd done it all by myself.

That day I was able to stop binge eating from creeping its way into my evening. Before getting help, I don't think I would have even tried to stop the surge. I don't think I *could have* tried. I was weak, easily tempted and controlled by my eating disorder. I knew help was out there, but I didn't even know how to start putting myself into the position to get help. I knew I needed it, and that was as far as I'd gotten.

*Can I handle the extravagant cheat meal tonight? And then can I handle the excessive guilt that will come when I finish binge eating? Can I make the guilt go away tomorrow by eating as little as possible? Will that balance it out?*

Of course, my answer to those racing questions was always "yes."

Eating disorder management comes with an extent to which you give up control and also maintain control. You have to give up the extreme, unwarranted analyzing of what you put into your body. But you also have to control eating habits that take you to a dark place. You have choices to make—choices to keep you in a healthy place—and you certainly have to control those decisions.

But what if you slip up? What if you lapse?

Then you get right to your self-care practice, and you use self-care to alleviate the guilt and anger felt from a mistake. And that, friends, is called forgiveness.

Rely on your ability to forgive yourself for making the mistake. Forgive yourself for having an eating disorder and for losing one small fight.

Let's face it—guilt cannot kill you. Stand up to that guilt and be mightier than blame. Let go of anger and love yourself instead.

Think about a time when you were a child—a time when you were an unstoppable kid full of excitement, mischief, innocence and bravery.

Now think about a time when you made a mistake and "got in trouble." Maybe your grades dropped, maybe you didn't clean your room when told, maybe you acted up at the dinner table, or maybe you threw a senseless temper tantrum. Sure, you probably got a spanking (if you grew up like I did), or were put in timeout or grounded by your parents or guardians. But you were able to return to your source of punishment and they still loved you just as much. And even though you let your parents or guardians down, their love for you was unconditional—unwrinkled, unblemished and as resilient as ever.

You have to break through anger and break down the make-believe barriers keeping you from love within yourself. **You have to give yourself unconditional love in eating disorder management.**

Try the following exercise, which is borrowed from Day 10: I Choose to Love Myself Today of Gabby Bernstein's book *May Cause Miracles.*

Choosing to love yourself is the only choice you have if you want to avoid fearful thoughts of self-hate, disappointment and anger. If you want to ensure unconditional love for yourself, you will have to communicate that message through a devoted practice.

"What you say about yourself unconsciously becomes what you consciously believe about yourself," Bernstein writes in her guide's Week 2: A New Self-Perception.

For the exercise, having a box of tissues handy might be a good idea.

- Find a mirror and take the mirror to a comforting place within your home.
- Look directly into the mirror until you find the reflection of your eyes. Look into them. Look into yourself.

- Now say, "I love you."
- Repeat several times, and maintain your gaze. Stare right into your own eyes and your inner self.
  - "I love you."
  - "I love you."
  - "I love you."

Let go of anything holding you back. Open the sluicegates. Allow any emotions that enter your heart to flood it from its core.

"This exercise may bring up several emotions, maybe some you feel totally unprepared for," Bernstein writes. "Affirming self-love in the mirror was the opposite of what I'd been taught to do, and it made me feel almost embarrassed."

Release your entire self. Don't judge how you feel. Allow yourself to experience any feeling that may occur in its natural state—don't try to change sensations you experience and allow your passions to just be.

Open your heart and let love take over—unconditional love for who you are completely—with or without an eating disorder.

I've always thought, based on fear, that I'm not easy-going and that I should be easy-going. Realistically, an easy-going personality is not as prevalent in me as it is in others. And that's OK. Just because I'm not easy-going doesn't mean that I should fix something to become easy-going. Even though easy-going sounds like an ideal characteristic to have, I love myself unconditionally and embrace my intense drive. Without that drive, perhaps I'd never have written the first word of this book.

I've also believed that something must be wrong with me because I'm always anxious. I'm now (sometimes) able to see through this lie and know that I might be anxious and there is nothing wrong with me. Perhaps anxiety is to thank for keeping me on the strict editing schedule needed to complete this book.

Thank goodness for the recent introduction of the cucumber emoji on smartphones. Pamela texts them to me when she knows I need a reminder to be cool. Cool as a cucumber … or three cucumbers. Pamela's cucumber emojis usually come in three's. She knows one might not be enough!

With each day that I'd no longer attended treatment at the EDTC, I stumbled into opportunities to start thinking about sharing my eating disorder experience with others. Assumptions, beliefs and ideals some people had about eating disorders were real eye-openers.

So let's get one thing very clear, here: **You cannot tell from the outside whether someone has an eating disorder**. Your neighbor could have one, and until you hear their story or see their behavioral struggle firsthand, you'll never know. You cannot make an unfair judgment based on what you see on the outside.

Looking back on my very first phone call to the EDTC, I feel foolish remembering that I told the gentleman on the line that "you'd never know I struggle with eating and that I binge eat."

*What did I even mean by that? That just because I maintained muscle tone, my eating disorder was hidden out of sight? That my eating disorder was unperceivable because of my outer appearance?*

If only I knew back then what I'd learned during treatment.

I would have known that an eating disorder is an *internal* thing. The external features, appearance and size of a person in no way indicates an eating disorder. In fact, my peers at the EDTC and I represented a diverse group of folks. No one "looked" like they had an eating disorder. No one acted like they struggled. It wasn't until we got to know each other that we had any idea of each other's unique battles with food, and from there we could compassionately lend support.

An eating disorder, according to the EDTC, is a very difficult aspect of someone's life. It's a condition that fails to reflect someone's true values.

An eating disorder is multi-determined, which means it can surface in various ways from person to person. Eating disorders are "rooted in a genetic vulnerability," and so a person can be at a higher risk for the development of the disorder than his or her societal peers.

The EDTC says that as a result of environmental stressors and similar factors, people at high risk may likely experience the onset and development of a disorder. The disorder's symptoms can come in numerous forms and functions from person to person.

"For some," the EDTC says, "eating disorder symptoms may give an individual a sense of management over feelings and controlling difficulties in his or her life. Some of these difficulties may include developing a sense of self, managing emotions, and navigating challenges in work and relationships."

In the journey toward eating disorder management, you grow closer to health restoration so that you can be your best you, and you can govern challenges and acquire a sturdy sense of who you are, according to your individual values and beliefs you hold dear.

⇒

Now let's get another thing even clearer: **You won't feel differently whether you have an eating disorder or not.**

Instead of feeling the existence of an eating disorder inside of you, accept that it's there, and that oftentimes the disorder is so dormant that it might even seem to have vanished. It's a certain type of mental health monster that likes to jump out and scare you, as if it were waiting for you to turn the corner into darkness.

It's a monster that you have to be ready to face. By recognizing your strengths, you can use those powers as ammunition when your eating disorder decides to attack.

For example, grab a piece of paper and jot down some of your transferrable skills—in other words, things you're good at doing. If you're like me, your top transferrable skills include **critical thinking, organizing, presenting, speaking and editing.**

How do those skills relate to managing your eating disorder?

Start by thinking of how you feel when your eating disorder starts to creep into your life.

Next, think of what you can do to prevent a lapse or relapse.

Last, create a way that each talent can be bigger, stronger and more powerful than your eating disorder.

*When I start to feel triggered by my eating disorder, I feel anxious, scared, weak, guilty and wretched.*

*I call on my **critical thinking** skills to help keep me safe from a lapse or relapse and fight off eating disorder behaviors. Critical thinking awakens the mind, fuels brainpower and deepens understanding of facts versus false judgment.*

Critical thinking will lead me to see evidence instead of F.E.A.R.–based beliefs by sparking my mind to think in new ways and expand its current assessment of my eating disorder's tempting pressure.

My eating disorder is weaker than my soul. I run my life. I can and will be healthy.

*I call on my* **organizing** *skills to help keep me safe from a lapse or relapse and fight off eating disorder behaviors. Organization maintains orderly association of mental thoughts, urges, behaviors and health.*

Organizing will help me keep my thoughts laid out in a clear, logical manner that will arrange emotions and urges and control responsive behaviors.

I will divide my eating disorder thoughts into groups and arrange them in order of strength—from easiest to fight to most difficult to face. I will step back and recognize the emotions each urge is causing inside me. I will stay in control of each group and make sure no trigger is strong enough to win as I fight each urge in the order in which I placed it.

*I call on my* **presentation** *skills to help keep me safe from a lapse or relapse and fight off eating disorder behaviors. Presentation allows me to confront the trigger head on and lay out a dominating, undefeatable battle plan.*

Presentation skills accelerate my performance, meaning I'll be able to act in a healthy way.

Presenting my willpower, knowledge and best self will take the power away from the eating disorder and keep the ball in my court. I will present a person (me) who is stronger than an eating disorder and maintain that persona when confronted with eating disorder urges. My refined practice will carry me above my eating disorder's reach.

*I call on my* **speaking** *skills to keep me safe from a lapse or relapse and fight off eating disorder behaviors. A strong, clear voice empowers me to speak over my eating disorder.*

By talking out loud, even screaming at my eating disorder, I have the power to send it packing before it has the chance to impact my choices.

Speaking confidently from my soul asserts that my eating disorder is smaller than I am. When I speak out loud to my eating disorder urges, I am no longer moved or shaken. My speaking skills convince my eating disorder that it doesn't have a chance in hell. And I won't shut up until I get my way.

*I call on my **editing** skills to help keep me safe from a lapse or relapse and fight off eating disorder behaviors. Editing finds errors, recommends revisions and is necessary for a flawless final product.*

By editing the triggers that cause my eating disorder's F.E.A.R.–based emotions, I will tweak them into truths that disprove the need to binge eat.

If I edit the temptation caused by an eating disorder, I will bring it back down to its actual size—a size too small to handle my willpower and drive. I will oversee my eating disorder's fury and rewrite it so it's absent of wrath and rage.

With that reflection on my strengths and transferrable skills, I realized my F.E.A.R.–based thought that I wasn't ready to leave EDTC treatment was absolutely false and my discharge came at a time when I could start managing my eating disorder without the help of treatment sessions. The EDTC saw progress and strength in me that I'd buried in fear.

# CHAPTER 25

# Three Weeks
# Post Treatment
### *Wednesday, September 27*

Since getting help for my eating disorder and completing Intensive Outpatient treatment at the EDTC, I've surprisingly maintained the same feeling of self-pressure and demand for "being on"—the need for uninterrupted concentration and unpleasant heaviness that the EDTC had implanted inside of me along my journey toward recovery.

Shouldn't the pressure have calmed down and somewhat withered away by now, three weeks past the big finish line? Or is all this pressure happening because of my personality type, and it's just part of who I am although at the end of the day, it's really unnecessary? The pressure stems from lies I subconsciously tell myself when in reality freedom is, and can be, my truth. Instead of coaching myself on the need to improve, I should coach myself on recognizing and living with the condition of being efficient enough and good enough.

Well, folks, the secret sauce is doing the work and committing to practice. Intensive Outpatient treatment is indeed called "intensive" for a reason. It's not about keeping you comfortable. It's about effectively reaching recovery and staying in a healthy, victorious, imperfect place.

I feel smarter when it comes to living with an eating disorder. I've received education that enables me to better handle mental health stress and eating disorder triggers.

I'm also more prepared to fight any urges and unhealthy temptations that come my way. I now have plenty of ammunition in my back pocket to get the best of an eating disorder urge before it gets the best of me, and so I feel more powerful. I feel stronger and braver, as though

I'm a soldier prepared for combat, fully equipped with adequate gear and a survival kit, and if I do fall off an eating disorder cliff, I now have a T-11 parachute to deliver me to safety.

I'll never forget the painful experiences my eating disorder took me through—feeling like I'd reached my last breath and feeling like my eyelids could permanently close, my body become stiff and cold. Those scary moments are too dark and too frightening to escape my memory's confinement. The scar on my soul is permanent, but with time and continued work to heal, my hope is that the scar will eventually fade.

Healing takes work well beyond the EDTC's doors and into the future.

I now have enough faith needed to never resort to an all-out, incapacitating, agonizing binge-eating episode ever again.

If I were to endure another uncontrollable binge-eating episode, the food would feel like poison as it passes through my body because I'd be reminded of the incident—in July 2017—when my eating disorder took me way too close to a death scare.

Simply put, the memories are too horrific to revisit and I can never let myself go there again.

I've worked too hard to find strength, and I've thankfully made too much progress to allow another severe, dangerous binge-eating episode to strike. I'm fiercely on guard, ready to take it down, and ready to take it out.

The work required during the healing process is SUPPOSED to be intense. You're going through a lot of change! You're transforming your life in a beautiful, wild and free way ... but ... that doesn't mean you'll feel beautiful, wild and free every minute of every day going forward.

You will be taken to your threshold and you will break down. And that's where transformation happens and where you break through to a healthier, happier life.

*"If it doesn't challenge you, it doesn't change you."—Fred DeVito*

*As executive vice president of movement classes + training at exhale spa, Fred leads training for Core Fusion teachers at 18 exhale locations, and he oversees the training program's quality and efficiency that, as of*

*November 2017, includes just over 120 teachers and a student monthly membership of more than 30,000.*

Fred's someone I've admired since meeting him in 2013, when all because of one tweet from me, he taught a morning barre class at the midtown Atlanta exhale spa to fit my work schedule of noon to 9 p.m. I did what anyone who's active on social media would do—I just asked.

Only through intensive therapy can you learn to manage arduous physical and mental health problems and disorders. Therapeutic programs like those offered at the EDTC challenge you to become more self-aware, become clear about your goals and authentic values, build your ability to cope, gain and enrich your self-esteem, improve communication skills, and boost your knack of pointing out, normalizing and conveying your passions.

Nobody said it would be easy. Mastery isn't constructed overnight. It's a practice that can very well last a lifetime.

The abusive patterns that accompany an eating disorder haunt people for long periods of time. It takes hard, hard work to break those patterns and find new ways.

Acceptance of the hard work produced the realization that fear led me to believe I shouldn't find it so difficult to relax. Truth be told, hitting the pause button and taking a couple deep breaths will take me to a "good enough" state of relaxation, even if that doesn't mean my travelling mind is perfectly still. I can relax while my thoughts wander.

What contributes to the onset of eating disorder symptoms and how can you better understand these events? Getting ahead of the eating disorder game and getting out in front of what causes it is so incredibly difficult and wearisome. It's a long, daunting process to grab ahold of recovery and make it yours, and the deep treatment, grit, grind and growth are without a doubt INTENSE.

Plus, as instructed by the EDTC therapists, there is no "perfect" recovery or "perfect" way to recover. Victories and success come in all shapes and sizes too.

Needs and achievements are unique from patient to patient, survivor to survivor.

For me, successful recovery means acceptance of life as-is, with no need or desire to modify any aspect of my life.

My health now lives in a new light: **Nutrition is more important than external appearance and how *I think I feel* on the inside.** It's like I've chosen to drink a different Kool-Aid—a Kool-Aid that's free of toxins that cause body dimorphic issues, F.E.A.R.–based anxiety and loyalty to perfectionism.

Recovery also provides a platform on which I can look at food differently. So far, that platform has made it much easier to decide which foods to eat. I've been able to breathe a little easier and to let go of *some* of the anxiety caused by food: which foods to eat and which foods not to eat.

It's about seeing food through a different lens—perhaps a lens you've never looked through, or a lens you lost a long time ago. Seeing food differently can work wonders in creating freedom to eat as you choose and maintain nutrition, meal to meal, snack to snack.

For example, breads and pastas are no longer seen as foods that cause bloating and weight gain, as their bad reputations have come to claim. Breads and pastas aren't "bad" foods. Instead, breads and pastas are sources of nutrition: essential nutrients in the form of vitamins, minerals, fiber and energy for your body.

One of those minerals is selenium and according to Sylvie Tremblay, MSc, cancer researcher and neuroscientist, selenium puts antioxidant enzymes into action, helping to keep your cells safe from molecular harm. Tremblay says the mineral manganese that's found in pasta assists your body in metabolizing carbohydrates and regulating blood sugar levels.

Tremblay says the folate in pasta (commonly known as vitamin B-9) helps develop red blood cells and expedites rapid cell growth. Pasta is also good for your vision, thanks to its carotenoids, lutein and zeaxanthin. The carotenoids help fight lung cancer too.

Pasta isn't the only nutritious food with a bad reputation. A burger is nutritious!

No longer should you see a burger as a fattening, inflammatory-causing, driver of heart disease. A burger is not a "bad" food. Instead, a burger is a food that provides protein, vitamins and minerals.

In fact, you'll consume almost 26 grams of protein in a patty that's 80 percent lean, according to health writer Sandi Busch.

Talk about taking your vitamins—get ready for this list: Vitamin B12, B6, niacin, folate, Vitamin E, Vitamin K and thiamine.

Vitamin B alone has quite the job to do. Important in the production of new red blood cells, Vitamin B makes sure enough oxygen is delivered throughout your body.

The list of minerals is even longer: zinc, selenium, phosphorous, iron, potassium, copper and magnesium.

And now for my personal favorite Fear Food that also carries a bad reputation among dieters: pizza. The classic cheese pizza. Stop seeing pizza as a fattening, high-carb, quick access pass for weight gain.

Instead, look at cheese pizza as a food that's highly helpful in filling your daily protein requirements, enabling your body to build amino acids, and helping keep your tissues and organs in top-notch shape.

Pizza contains phosphorous, which is essential for bone heath, dental health and maintaining energy, says Emily DeLacey, nutrition and dietetics expert.

DeLacey also points to pizza for its incredible calcium content. Eating the proper amount of calcium helps maintain strong bones and slow the process of bone loss as you age.

"Calcium is used to help the muscles in your body contract, including your heartbeat!" DeLacey adds.

At the end of the day, I'm not encouraging you to run out and eat all the breads, pasta, burgers and pizza you can get your hands on. What I'm telling you to do is to let go of the bad associations you hold onto when it comes to Fear Foods and all foods that cause you to feel guilt after eating them.

Since treatment, I've been able to gradually incorporate more Fear Foods into my diet—mostly due to the removal of mental labels and judgment and getting rid of expectations. Fear Foods no longer turn a meal into a "cheat meal" because of the "bad" components the meal contains. Instead, the meal is simply a meal that I chose, which happens to include bread, or pasta, or a burger, or a pizza. Without the label of "good" or "bad" on these meals—without any judgment at all—I'm able to consume the meal and accept the meal for what it gives me: nutrition and, most likely, the enjoyment of good taste.

**When you take away expectations, you have nothing to base judgments on**—food and in all areas of life. Once expectations no longer exist, there are no longer any standards, no more good or bad, no better or best.

No meal has to be categorized as good or bad, or better than the next meal, or the best meal you could possibly eat. It is, quite simply, the meal that is the meal.

Within the last week, my family and I ordered the food that was always my go-to for a big binge: pizza for dinner to eat while a college football game was being shown on TV. I finished two cheese sticks as an appetizer, then ate three slices of cheese pizza and finished the meal off with a serving of frozen yogurt.

The pizza was splendidly satisfying, perhaps because it was paired with a cozy night in, but I forced myself to literally stare at the pizza boxes and convince myself that I was full, that I didn't need to binge, and that sometime in the future, I'd have pizza again.

Since stripping judgment away from food, it's much easier to maintain portion control. If the food I eat is no longer "good" or "bad," I'm able to stop analyzing food selection and enjoy a healthy serving of whatever I might be eating at any given moment. Knowing that I'm not approaching a "bad" food or a "cheat meal" creates comfort in knowing that what used to be Fear Food will be available again, and so I don't have to binge eat it during that sitting. Enjoy a healthy portion at that time, and then repeat enjoyment of the healthy portion whenever you might eat that food again.

There's no "cheat meal," no "last binge meal," and no anxiety associated with guilt or even risk.

It's about enjoying a healthy portion of balanced foods that are appetizing, and seeing the good that comes from it: nutrition, delight, satisfaction and freedom.

And yes, other "culprits" like French fries, fried chicken and ice cream are also oh, so good to go!

Recovery and success mean living without judgment—judgment of myself and judgment of others. Instead, it means loving myself and loving others, unconditionally without question.

Recovery is about being authentic and doing what works for you, instead of giving people what you think they want. You'll find success in loving yourself in the form that works for you no matter what anyone else might want or what you think they want.

Recovery is about living through the good days and the bad days too. It's about gliding over the peaks, coasting along the plateaus, and graciously wading through the valleys, never losing sight of your values, your hopes and your dreams.

Recovery and success mean living without pressure, making choices without a challenge and breathing without burdens.

Recovery and success mean living in the gray area, where everything is OK—perfectly just OK—gray and OK.

**Recovery: in my heart, in my mind, shared with others.**

Now, three weeks after treatment, I choose to accept that I have what I need at this time: tools to get through, like trust in myself, strengthened relationships, deepened commitment and nurtured awareness. I don't have the perfect solution to forever fix my mental health once and for all, and there is no such thing as a perfect solution.

I have exactly what I need to get by and be at peace with my eating disorder, and to continue a fulfilled life of happiness, laughter and accomplishment of more goals than I can count. And, most important, love.

*I will look forward. I will look forward.*
*YOU will look forward. YOU will look forward.*

# Epilogue

There's a phrase that, until just very recently, always made me cringe. Even made me angry.

"Trust the journey."

I've never wanted to embark on or enjoy the journey, let alone trust it. Others might find these three words a motivating mantra, an encouraging affirmation, or a reminder just to keep on keepin' on.

But I hated the message. I couldn't even hear it spoken aloud without snarling the left side of my top lip, rolling my eyes and letting out a growling sigh of disgust.

Because the journey, as I'd somehow come to believe, implied a prolonged length of time, strenuous effort and maybe even a total transformation before making the goal mine. It's not the hard work, the going to great lengths or the dedication that bothered me. It was the steps I'd have to take and the endurance that came with each phase.

Patiently taking steps meant time in the gray area. Defining a goal and achieving it ASAP was the good ol' black-and-white way of going about things. I wanted the instant gratification and sense of accomplishment. And I wanted them *now*.

I'd forgotten that the journey, no matter its length or level of difficulty, could be a lot of fun, and that spending time working toward a goal is when real, treasured memories are made. It's not always about how quickly you cross the finish line, but what you do to make each mile count.

My mom and I ran "A Midsummer Night's Run 5K" together with neighborhood friends each year during my childhood. We never competed against anyone, nor did we care what the race clock said when we finished the last leg. We enjoyed the event regardless of the outcome.

Finally, I've come to realize that by trusting the journey, you learn lessons that will continue to fuel your fire for achieving great things all while developing empathy for yourself and others as you travel through life. Basically, it's the journey that teaches you to give yourself and others compassion and a well-deserved break.

The journey to recovery and beyond has enabled me to give others the unconditional love they deserve. From the time I began eating disorder treatment and applying my new understandings to all parts of life, I've been slowly pulling off the Band-Aids that have kept me from trusting myself, others, and so many things outside my realm of control.

It's OK to ask for help!

An eating disorder is a never-ending journey. A year after treatment, I still experience ups and downs, I still use the same therapeutic tools, and I still hold the same values when it comes to eating. I don't go on crash diets. I no longer have cheat meals, but I've eaten too much on a few occasions and those occasions didn't break me. I enjoy eating different foods and appreciate the nutrition all foods provide. I've found that balance is everything and my most reliable tool for staying healthy.

**My mom and I ran "A Midsummer Night's Run 5k" through downtown Lexington, Kentucky, in July 1992.**

When tough times go down, it's easier to understand and accept that I don't know, right then and there, when things will get better. They probably won't get better immediately, so there's no point to rush to fix anything. Trusting the journey makes it easier to accept the condition as-is, and to acknowledge the setback as something that's manageable instead of a disaster that ruins everything. Trusting the journey is the ability to roll with the punches.

The more tools you have handy, the more equipped you are to overcome those punches. Of the tools gained from treatment at the EDTC, I still rely on urge surfing most of all to keep me on track. When I feel an urge to control my eating, I pause with the urge and ask myself questions, which helps me recognize the truth and rise above the urge's deception.

- Do I REALLY want to overeat?
- Is the craving I'm having real?
- Why do I want to eat a certain way or eat a certain food; is it for a healthy reason?
- What will happen if I resist this urge?
- What's driving my feelings right now and what choices do I have?

By choosing not to immediately act on the urge, I'm able to assess the situation and make a healthy choice. Urge surfing has helped me build trust in the journey. In eating habits and in all areas of life, I've developed mental agility, resilience and a much-needed free spirit.

I am successful in overcoming an eating disorder, and furthermore, I live a happy life with continued success while accepting that struggles can haunt me any time, at any place. I've learned behaviors like coping mechanisms, stress reducers and mindfulness practices that keep me well, which operate almost like muscle memory. These skills are now in my toolkit and I can access them whenever I want. It's not about pushing the elephant out of the room, but learning how to share the space and live with it.

In eating and in just living my life, the gray has definitely, *finally* become OK.

The journey—my journey—has taught me to have gratitude. Gratitude for what feels good, but also for what doesn't.

The journey, no matter how impossible and repulsive it may have always seemed, has actually given me gifts and the realization that I have something very valuable to offer: an incredible story of survival.

# Index

Numbers in *bold italics* indicate pages with illustrations